Life and Death in the Executive Fast Lane

· ·

Manfred F. R. Kets de Vries

. . . .

Life and Death in the Executive Fast Lane

Essays on

Irrational Organizations

and Their Leaders

Jossey-Bass Publishers
San Francisco

Substantial discounts on bulk quantities of Jossey-Bass books are available to corporations, professional associations, and other organizations. For details and discount information, contact the special sales department at Jossey-Bass Inc., Publishers. (415) 433–1740; Fax (800) 605–2665.

For sales outside the United States, please contact your local Paramount Publishing International Office.

 Manufactured in the United States of America on Lyons Falls Pathfinder Tradebook. This paper is acid-free and 100 percent totally chlorine-free.

Library of Congress Cataloging-in-Publication Data

Kets de Vries, Manfred F. R.
    Life and death in the executive fast lane: essays on irrational organizations and their leaders/Manfred F. R. Kets de Vries.—1st ed.
      p. cm.—(The Jossey-Bass management series)
    Includes bibliographical references and index.
    ISBN 0-7879-0112-1
    1. Industrial management. 2. Leadership. I. Title. II. Series.
HD31.K462 1995
658.4'092—dc20   95-4952

FIRST EDITION
HB Printing 10 9 8 7 6 5 4 3 2 1

Contents

. . . .

Preface

. . . .

*He [the businessman] is the only man who is forever
apologizing for his occupation.*

H. L. Mencken

*The greatest difficulty in the world is not for people to
accept new ideas but to make them forget about their
old ideas.*

John Maynard Keynes

Anybody can hold the helm when the sea is calm.

Publilius Syrus

One way of describing my work—teaching at a major European
business school, writing, consulting, and working as a psychoanalyst—is to say that I try to combine the "dismal science" (John
Maynard Keynes's description of economics) with the "impossible
profession" (the name Sigmund Freud once gave to psychoanalysis).
I find that this dual way of looking at things can be quite powerful
when applied to the study of organizations. Using the two disciplines
together—surprising though it may seem at first—can give some
extremely useful insights into what makes organizations tick and into
why they, and the people within them, ultimately succeed or fail.

There is a lot to be said for putting people on the couch. It certainly facilitates the process of free association—saying anything

that comes to mind without observing the usual politesse of everyday life—and is a way of gaining insight into a person's conflicts, wishes, and motivations. Although it is impossible to put an entire organization on the couch, psychoanalysis is a useful metaphor in the study of how organizations function.

I should perhaps explain here the basis of my clinical approach to management. It rests on a number of premises, the first one being that all behavior is somehow determined. What at first glance may seem completely irrational may on closer inspection have an explanation and a deeper rationale. Moreover (and this may be perceived by some people as the real narcissistic injury), we are not aware of many of our wishes and fantasies; a considerable amount of our action and behavior appears to be unconscious.

In the last decade, an increasing number of people have realized the usefulness of applying clinical concepts (taken in particular from psychoanalysis, developmental psychology, cognition, family systems theory, and dynamic psychiatry) to organizational settings. Pioneers in this field, such as Abraham Zaleznik, Harry Levinson, and Elliott Jaques, have been followed by many others. These people are interested not only in the *how* but also in the *why*; they want to understand what is beyond the directly observable. They acknowledge that business is more about people than it is about the endless list of systems, procedures, and models so often found in management textbooks.

The crucial issue is whether the typical corporate executive really is a logical, dependable being. Is management in reality a rational task performed by rational people according to sensible organizational objectives? We all know better, yet the myth of rationality persists. In spite of all the evidence to the contrary, the notion that humans are rational decision makers has never lost its appeal. This notion has been advocated in economic theory and was also put forward by the time-and-motion man of the scientific management movement, Frederick Taylor. This movement, which favored management and organization by formulas, controls, and systems, can be seen as the forerunner of what today is called "professional" management.

Although there is undoubtedly something to be said for professional management, it sometimes takes a form in which style replaces substance and processes substitute for ideas and imagination. Supporters of this particular *Weltanschauung* build rigid structures and set up systems designed to make people behave predictably. They are sensitive to numbers and figures while treating people as anonymous entities. Most worrying of all is that their biggest threat seems to be creativity, since creativity risks introducing chaos and disorder into the systematized organization. In their desperate attempt to create order, proponents of professional management have taken humans out of the equation. Moreover, human playfulness has been completely forgotten. What must be truly frightening to these proponents is the discovery that so much of human behavior operates outside our direct awareness.

Many of the more rigid organizational theories have had their gestation in the ivory towers of academia, far removed from the day-to-day reality of organizational life. Perhaps more direct contact with the actual practitioners of management, and a better knowledge of their major personal and professional concerns, would give the theorists a greater awareness of what life in organizations is all about. Competitive analysis is certainly very important; structure and systems certainly matter; and job descriptions have a purpose—but so do people.

Those of us who have spent time in organizations know that senior executives can have an enormous influence on their organizations. They are the ones who differentiate their company from the competition; they influence the emerging vision and mission; they define the corporate culture; they create the structures and set strategy. As many have learned the hard way, a dysfunctional CEO not only makes life miserable for his or her staff but can affect a whole company's way of managing—affect it enough to contribute significantly to the organization's decline. In this context, it should be said that Freud's often-quoted dictum that a dream is the "royal road to the unconscious" has a wider application than he originally intended. The road to understanding the dynamics of organizational life is often dependent on understanding what might be termed the "inner theater" of its key executives: the patterns of conduct that guide their behavior.

What is this inner theater? How do an individual's core conflictual relationship themes affect his or her behavior? What are the pervasive themes that define a person and that remain basically the same whatever the situation may be? I have tried to answer some of these questions in the essays included in this book. Wise executives will ask themselves the same questions, although it will quickly become obvious that pursuing these issues is not easy. It can take a lot of effort to find out what is behind the façade displayed to the outside world; but it can be done, and it is worthwhile.

How can it be done? In my own teaching, consulting, and therapeutic work, I push executives to become organizational detectives. I want them to learn how to look beyond the obvious to find the deeper meaning of certain actions. I want them to understand that they sometimes get into trouble because of unconscious processes that they neither see, understand, nor accept.

One way for an executive to gain insight into his or her own inner theater is to study other business leaders and their companies, to make sense out of their behavior and actions. In order to help potential executives arrive at this kind of understanding, I make frequent use of case studies in my classes, sometimes accompanied by video material. Leaders such as Jack Welch, Percy Barnevik, Carlo de Benedetti, Richard Branson, André Citroen, Coco Chanel, Walt Disney, Roberto Calvi, Refaat El-Sayed, and Ernest Saunders are the subject of case studies I use in the classroom.

To set the investigative process in motion, I ask the students leading questions. For example, why did the first Henry Ford of the Ford Motor Company stick to the Model T for nineteen years in spite of changing market conditions and an enormous drop in market share? Why did he behave so erratically? When his engineers presented him with a slightly modified version of the Model T, he flew into a tantrum and kicked the car apart. Why? What made him so unwilling to change the car? What was the symbolic meaning of the car to him? Why did he unleash a reign of terror in the company, employing henchmen such as Harry Bennett, a person with tight connections to the Detroit underworld? What lay behind Ford's strange political activities, his isolationism, and his anti-Semitism? Why did he never appreciate his son Edsel's efforts to steer the company back on course? And what was it, despite all these quirks, that made him such a visionary? After all, he was the first person really to recognize the value of using the assembly line to make a mass-produced car at a time when consumer trends were pointing in the opposite direction. What were his inner psychic needs and conflicts, his hopes and desires, and the forces that drove him to act the way he did? What differentiated him from other people? What made him such an innovator?[1]

These are the kinds of questions that I raise not only in MBA classes but also in my work with executives. Gradually, students and seminar participants arrive at a clearer idea of what kind of person Ford was, the nature of his interpersonal relationships, and how his style affected the organization. They begin to realize the extent to which his behavior in the Ford Motor Company was colored by his personal history and to what degree Ford was a prisoner of his past.

Interestingly enough, like most young medical students, class participants begin to see the symptoms of similar patterns of behavior in themselves. At times this may be frightening, but the process of recognition generally makes them think. In my experience, this learning process triggers self-reflection and insight. As future "masters of the universe," to quote Thomas Wolfe's *Bonfire of the Vanities*, these fledgling consultants, entrepreneurs, investment bankers, and industrialists may later profit from this approach. It gives them some insight into the processes of power, authority, and influence and suggests why we should be concerned about them. With luck, class participants also realize how easily they themselves could get stuck in a vicious circle and become prisoners of their own past. Understanding these processes may make young leaders more aware of the extent to which certain types of organizations may adversely affect their mental or even physical health.

Plays such as Arthur Miller's *Death of a Salesman* and films such as Orson Welles's *Citizen Kane*, Sidney Lumet's *Twelve Angry Men*, Ingmar Bergman's *Wild Strawberries*, and Woody Allen's *The Other Woman* can provide students with further insight into what makes a person or an organization tick. This sort of material is quite different from the number-crunching that students are exposed to in other courses. The right side of the brain—the part responsible for more intuitive processes—is not exactly nurtured at management schools; and as a result, honest self-examination is not a skill students work to develop.

In the following essays, I have also drawn on a seminar on leadership that I have been teaching for a number of years at INSEAD— a very unusual program, different from all the others I participate in, which centers on the *life* case study. Spending three intensive weeks (spread out over a period of six months) working with twenty very senior executives, discussing their lives, their major concerns, their fears, and their efforts to change their lives, is an emotionally draining experience for both teacher and participants. The exercise of mutual problem solving, combined with a mirroring process in which participants are brought firmly up against the image others have of them, can be dramatically powerful. The discovery that people are not alone in facing a particular type of problem, that they are not that different from other people, can counteract frequently intense feelings of isolation and give a sense of reintegration with the human race.

In my clinical work, I am often struck by the number of people who fail to realize the extent to which there is a continuity between our past, our present, and our future. These people make the same mistakes over and over again because they are unable to recognize repetitive patterns in their behavior that have become dysfunctional. They are stuck in a vicious circle and do not know how to get out. The Danish philosopher Kierkegaard expressed the sadness and poignancy of this when he said that the tragedy of life is that while we can understand it only backward, we have to live it forward.

Freud once told the novelist Stefan Zweig that all his life he had been "struggling with the demon"—the demon of irrationality. Wise organizational analysts have to do the same. Organizations that fail to pay attention to these demons will miss vital signs of weakness in the system and will lose out in the global competitive game.

My aim in demonstrating the use of the clinical paradigm has been to open the eyes of organizational participants, to make them realize what can and cannot be done, to recognize their strengths and weaknesses, to prevent executives from getting stuck in vicious circles, and to make them understand the causes of resistance to change. My intention has been to widen their choice. Is that not what mental health is all about?

The essays in this book do not emphasize such aspects of formal organizations as infra- and superstructure, job descriptions, and span of control. Instead, they explore the underlying structures of the organization: corporate culture, group dynamics, the nature of interpersonal relationships, emotional experiences, and individual motivation.

This perspective will appeal to five major audiences. First and foremost, it will be of interest to business practitioners who want to deepen their understanding of organizational culture, leadership style, career dynamics, stress, and the individual-organization interface in general.

For academics, this book will provide another view of human motivation and action in organizations. It will be useful as supplementary reading both for undergraduate and for graduate courses in organizational behavior, industrial and organizational psychology, management theory, public administration, and human resource management. It is also suitable for students of political science, sociology, psychology, social work, and government.

By contributing to a better understanding of the personal and interpersonal processes at work in the organization, this book will assist human resource management professionals in designing effective selection, reward, appraisal, planning, and development systems and will help them to align these systems more closely with organizational reality.

Management consultants can use this book to increase the effectiveness of their organizational diagnosis and intervention. The insights provided by the essays will also be helpful in the consulting practice.

Finally, certain mental health professionals, such as industrial and organizational psychologists, industrial social workers, occupational psychiatrists, and clinical organizational psychologists, can use ideas from this book to assist their clients in diffusing irrational behavior and stress in organizations.

I have divided the book into two parts. The emphasis in the first group of essays is on organizational issues, while the role of the *person* takes on a more central focus in the second part of the book. I must admit, however, that the dividing line between these two parts is a rather arbitrary one, as individual and organizational issues are part of an intricately woven tapestry.

That being said, we will begin with the journey, if I may call it that, of the organization itself through the many potential events and crises that shape it.

Acknowledgments

First, I would like to thank my patients, students, and clients for helping me in developing my ideas. Nothing is more stimulating than puzzling questions to an "archeologist" of the mind who tries to make sense of what seem like riddles. I also want to express my gratitude to Jurriaan Kamp, former editor of the Dutch daily *NRC/ Handelsblad*, whose request that I contribute a regular column for his newspaper got this project under way. Writing for a mass public as opposed to a highly specialized audience was an extremely interesting learning experience. In addition, I want to thank Sophia Acland and Eva Svenstedt for their editorial assistance. The editorial contribution of Sally Simmons is particularly appreciated. As an editor's editor, she really knows how to shape language and clarify text that otherwise would have remained quite murky. My research assistant, Elizabeth Florent-Treacy, deserves my special gratitude. Her positive attitude toward my work has helped me in getting through many a low moment. She not only has been instrumental in organizing the manuscript but also has contributed editorially. In addition, she has corrected more drafts than I care to remember. I want to thank my secretary, Sheila Loxham, for playing a kindly Cerberus by protecting me from the pressures of "real life." I am also grateful to INSEAD's associate dean of research and development, Yves Doz, for his continued support for projects of this type. I would like to express the same appreciation for the present and former deans at INSEAD, Antonio Borges, Ludo Van der Heyden, and Claude Rameau. I owe a special debt to William Hicks of Jossey-Bass, who has always been a strong supporter of my work. Finally, last but certainly not least, I want to thank my wife, Elisabet, for being such a constructive critic and cheerleader.

Paris, France   Manfred F. R. Kets de Vries
June 1995

To my children
Eva, Fredrik, and Oriane
and our *smultronställen*
(our patches of wild strawberries)

The Author

· ·

Manfred F. R. Kets de Vries holds the Raoul de Vitry d'Avaucourt Chair of Human Resource Management at the European Institute of Business Administration (INSEAD), France, where he is clinical professor of management and leadership. He did a doctoral examination in economics (Econ. Drs.) at the University of Amsterdam (1966) and holds an ITP certificate (1967) from Harvard; in addition, he has a master's degree (1968) and a doctoral degree (1970) in business administration from the Harvard Business School. In 1977 he undertook psychoanalytic training at the Canadian Psychoanalytic Institute, and in 1982 he became a member of the Canadian Psychoanalytic Society and the International Psychoanalytic Association. He is a practicing psychoanalyst. He has held professorships at McGill University, the École des Hautes Études Commerciales, Montreal, and the Harvard Business School.

Kets de Vries's main research interest lies in the interface between psychoanalysis, dynamic psychiatry, and management. Specific areas of interest are leadership, cross-cultural management, career dynamics, organizational stress, entrepreneurship, family businesses, and the psychological systems that make for corporate transformation and change. Kets de Vries's books include *Power and the Corporate Mind* (1975, 1985, with Abraham Zaleznik), *Organizational Paradoxes: Clinical Approaches to Management* (1980, 1994), *The Irrational Executive: Psychoanalytic Explorations in Management*

(1984, editor), *The Neurotic Organization: Diagnosing and Changing Counter-Productive Styles of Management* (1984, 1990, with Danny Miller), *Unstable at the Top* (1988, with Danny Miller), *Prisoners of Leadership* (1989), *Handbook of Character Studies* (1991, with Sidney Perzow), *Organizations on the Couch* (1991), and *Leaders, Fools, and Impostors* (1993). In addition, Kets de Vries has published over one hundred scientific papers as either articles or chapters in books, and his books and papers have been translated into ten languages. He has written numerous case studies, including three that have been named best European case of the year.

Kets de Vries is a member of many editorial boards and a founding member of the International Society for the Psychoanalytic Study of Organizations. He is also a newspaper columnist and a consultant on organizational design/transformation and strategic human resource management, and he has done extensive executive development work with many U.S., Canadian, European, and Asian companies. He has five times received INSEAD's distinguished teacher award.

Part I

. . . .

Leaders and the Organization

My purpose in this first group of essays is to present principles that can be used to decipher what really goes on in organizations. Apart from discussing some of the issues that are regularly encountered in organizational life, I have also tried to shed light on some of the underlying dimensions. I have tried to indicate how to make sense out of specific behaviors, stories, myths, rituals, jokes, and other aspects of organizational culture and to help people understand the conflicts, anxieties, defenses, and tensions that are part and parcel of organizational life.

I hope, however, that readers will not fall into the trap of simple causality in applying these principles. Although I have been trying to bring "humans" back into the organization, that does not mean that all organizational problems are simply derivatives of the pathology of a company's leadership. To put leaders on the couch will not necessarily resolve organizational dysfunction. Leaders do not operate in isolation. There is an external environment that has to be taken into consideration. Although leaders can create sick organizations, forces in the environment can also adversely affect organizational participants. It is an extremely complex, mutually interactive process.

It seems logical to begin, in Chapter One, with an overview of leadership. Leaders have two roles to fill—charismatic and instrumental. The first role encompasses how they envision, empower, and energize their followers. In their instrumental role, leaders are organizational architects. They structure, design, and control their organization, and they reward followers' behavior. These two roles are the basis of effective leadership, as we shall see.

It is one thing to describe the role of the leader in theory; it is quite another to put it into practice. Chapter Two looks at executives who take on the role of leader in their organization, either coming in as outsiders or arriving through internal promotion. They must implement their charismatic and instrumental roles as quickly as possible—and often in the face of opposition from all sides. This essay covers many of the conflicting issues and interests of which the new CEO must be aware.

Adapting to a new leader is only one of the significant processes that an organization is likely to undergo. Staying competitive implies change, and that often means increasing or reducing the size of the organization and the workforce. Yet change is painful. Even positive change can be far more stressful than people realize. Chapters Three and Four examine difficult changes, such as downsizing, and the more positive processes of mergers and acquisitions. How does an effective leader accommodate followers' negative reactions? How can a top executive tap into the competitive advantages of change? In order to make change work, a regard for the human side of the process is essential.

Corporate culture, which is a kind of codification of that human side, can be a make-or-break factor in times of organizational change. It can be seen as the glue that holds a company together and is an influential control system in global organizations. Chapter Five provides clues for decoding the essentials of corporate culture—symbols, language, and behavior—and for changing them.

Recognizing differences in national culture is just as important as considering differences in corporate culture. Cross-border mergers and acquisitions are prime example of events in which national culture can play a determining role. In Chapter Six, the issue of diversity in cultural attitudes toward work is addressed.

In today's global business climate, it is likely that top executives will find themselves working not only with colleagues of different nationalities but also in foreign countries. Unfortunately, 20 to 50 percent of them will return home early. International executives obviously require sensitivity to both corporate and national cultures. Few organizations seem to realize, however, the importance of adequately preparing the executive and his or her spouse and family for the move. In addition, many executives encounter problems with repatriation, finding that there is no job waiting for them upon their return. Chapter Seven discusses ways to make expatriation and repatriation constructive experiences for executives and their organization.

Borderless corporations are providing a new organizational model for the future. Companies such as ASEA Brown Boveri (ABB) operate globally and act locally. With the increase in global companies, there is a need for truly global leaders. Are such leaders born or made? Using examples such as the Dalai Lama and Percy Barnevik, Chapter Eight examines factors that assist in the development of a global leader from childhood on.

It is important to bear in mind that the business practices discussed in Chapters One through Eight can be called excellent *at present*, but even the best practices may become virtually useless if they are not continually adapted to anticipate future trends. What, then, are the new trends in management? More important, which are valid and which are just the flavor of the month? Chapter Nine concludes Part One by discussing how business will be conducted in the future and predicting the areas in which companies will need to excel.

In these essays, I have tried to combat magical thinking, to make people realize that certain organizational problems tend to be deeply rooted and extremely resistant to change in spite of what many snake-oil salespeople disguised as organizational consultants try to tell their clients. Although the realization of people's strong resistance to change may be painful, and some illusions will be shattered, the sense of realism that results from such thinking may well be worth it.

. . . .

If I'm the Leader, Will Anyone Follow?
A Definition of Leadership

*Leadership is the ability to get men to do what they
don't like to do and like it.*

Harry Truman

Better to reign in hell than serve in heaven.

John Milton

We are all worms, but I think that I am a glow worm.

Winston Churchill ·

What is being a leader all about? What are the key aspects of
the job? There is currently great interest in knowing more
about leadership, since many students of organizations argue that
companies are underled and overmanaged. What is needed, some
say, is more leadership.

Unfortunately, when we dive into the organizational literature
on leadership, we quickly become lost in a labyrinth: there are endless definitions, countless articles, and never-ending polemics.

The proliferation of literature on leadership is amply reflected by
the increase in the number of articles in its bible, the *Handbook of
Leadership*. While the old handbook, published in 1974, listed only
3,000 studies, that number increased to 5,000 within seven years and
has now passed the 7,000 mark. It is unfortunate that the popularity of leadership research has not been equaled by its relevance. The

titles of the theories—new and old—reveal the nature of that research: plodding and detached, far removed from the reality of day-to-day life. How many years of consideration versus structure studies of leadership are good for a person's mental health? Is it not an insult to one's intelligence to simplify leadership behavior to only two dimensions? Who really needs "vertical dyad" theories of leadership anyway? Will yet another laboratory study with students as guinea pigs give insight into what leaders really do? After all, what do undergraduate students know about such a complex phenomenon as leadership?

In the area of leadership, it seems that more and more has been studied about less and less. This trend prompted one wit to say recently that reading the current world literature on leadership is rather like going through a Parisian telephone directory written in Chinese!

Very briefly, it seems that most researchers would agree on a few obvious traits as being important for leaders. These are *conscientiousness, energy, intelligence, dominance, self-confidence, sociability, openness to experience, task-relevant knowledge*, and *emotional stability*. Beyond this, however, the myriad theories diverge, and it is easy to lose oneself in the academic hairsplitting.

But things are changing. A rebirth is taking place in the domain of leadership. A new group of researchers has come onto the scene—people who have moved out of the laboratory and, surprisingly enough, know what a leader looks like. They are interested in studying *real* business leaders.

What has undoubtedly helped this to come about is the proliferation of autobiographies by business leaders (admittedly penned, in most instances, with the help of a ghostwriter). After the autobiography of Chrysler's Lee Iacocca became a best-seller, it seemed as if every leader (and dollar-crazed publisher) felt the need to join the fray.

Present students of leadership are different. Not only have they branched out into the real world; their interest is in charismatic or transformational leaders, whom they are eager to differentiate from that peasant of organizational literature: the manager. With the kind of press the latter is getting, who wants to be a manager these days? The term *manager* has become almost a dirty word. Abraham Zaleznik, emeritus professor of leadership at Harvard, wrote an attention-grabbing article in the May/June 1977 *Harvard Business Review*, entitled "Managers and Leaders: Are They Different?" According to Zaleznik, the answer is yes. He argues that for managers, style seems to count more than substance and process more than reality. The implication is that this is not the type of person one needs. Obviously, in the brave new world of global business Olympics, we need leaders who can deal with change and keep abreast of competitive threats.

Of course, making a strong split between leaders and managers is a technique of highlighting certain differences. It is a way of simplifying an otherwise very complex world and as such can be useful. One could, for example, distinguish between managers and leaders by imagining a scale from one to ten that allows one to rate people on a number of categories.

But what categories could be used to highlight the differences? What specific themes are important? To start off, one could argue that leaders are more interested in the future, while managers stick to the present. Leaders are prepared to deal with change, while managers are more concerned about stability. Leaders focus on the long term, while managers are preoccupied by the short term. And leaders have vision and inspire others, while managers, lacking vision, have to be instructed. (It has been said that leaders do the right thing, while managers do things right.)

To continue this kind of classification, one could say that real leaders are driven people; their vision is influenced by a vivid inner theater. Leaders tend to externalize private motives and present them on a public stage. And of course their effectiveness in doing so depends on the historical moment—on whether the external environment is ready for their ideas.

Because of the way leaders touch people's lives, they are said to have charisma. The power base of managers, on the other hand, comes more from hierarchical authority. Leaders ask about *why*, while managers are more preoccupied with *how*. Leaders recognize the importance of corporate philosophy, core values, and shared goals, while managers see tactics, structure, and systems as more important. When making statements about mission and vision, leaders resort to simple language. They tend to have what we could call a helicopter view; they see the forest as well as the trees. By contrast, managers tend to muddle, making things complex. And leaders empower, while managers control. Leaders frequently resort to intuition, while managers are more concerned about logic. Finally, leaders go beyond pure corporate concerns, while for managers those are the only things that matter.

Looking at this scale, where do you find yourself? Are you weak or strong on leadership? Do you have what it takes?

As a matter of fact, this way of splitting the world is turning the manager into our new scapegoat. In real life, we need both qualities: a manager without leadership skills is a mere bureaucrat, while a visionary who does not know how to implement a vision will lead an organization astray.

Thus, looking at effective leaders, we can distinguish between two roles, both necessary. One is charismatic; the other, instrumental. Leaders need to envision the future and empower, energize, and motivate their followers. But leaders also have to structure, design, control, and reward behavior.

By *envision*, I mean that leaders must be effective in determining a direction in which to go and in building commitment to go in that direction. Leaders are the ones who say, "I want you to climb *this* mountain, not that one or that one." This vision is then the roadmap for all of those who come under their sphere of influence. It includes core values and beliefs, enabling leaders to define the guiding philosophy of the organization: the mission.

In making their vision and mission workable, leaders need to have a knack for perceiving salient trends in the environment. They must be attuned to many different kinds of information and gifted at creating a fit between their perceptions and the direction in which environmental forces are going.

Basically, leaders must be much better than other people at the whole process of managing cognitive complexity. Effective leaders are good at searching out and structuring the kind of information they need; their strength lies in making sense of an increasingly complex environment and then using the data obtained in problem solving. This talent manifests itself in their knack for simplification, for making highly complex issues palatable. Italian business leader Carlo de Benedetti is a good example of an individual who has used this talent to good effect. At meetings where other executives find themselves going around in circles, he can often incisively get to the heart of the matter.

If people are to be motivated, the mission statement needs to be inspirational. To talk merely about increasing the shareholders' wealth is not good enough. To say "We want to be fast imitators of other companies" also leaves something to be desired. The mission statement should be simple, yet it should stretch the mind of all the company's executives.

People in the political arena can be particularly good at articulating inspirational visions. Such people become inspirational because, when there is dissatisfaction with the existing status quo, they present an acceptable alternative and rally others around them to make that alternative happen. Think about Mahatma Gandhi's vision of an independent India, where Muslims and Hindus would live together in peace. Martin Luther King, Jr., had a vision of harmony between blacks and whites. John F. Kennedy, when he was president, had a very specific vision: he wanted someone on the moon by the end of the sixties. In the domain of business, we find Ingvar Kamprad of IKEA, who wants to make affordable furniture for the general public, while the Danish pharmaceutical company Novo Nordisk is trying to improve human life by preventing and treating diseases. Of course, not all visions are exemplary: there were the darker visions of Adolf Hitler's thousand-year *Reich*, for example.

It helps to have an enemy to focus on while enacting a mission. The more successful companies focus on their competitors. They want to know everything about their competitors so that they know how to build a base of attack. Think about the Pepsi and Coca-Cola wars. Remember Nike, Adidas, and Reebok? Likewise, Compaq and Dell seem to take pleasure out of destroying each other in their advertisements.

In focusing on a competitor, wise leaders build a base of attack just outside the market territory of the enemy. The trick is not to fight your competitor head on. Anybody who has ever participated in martial arts knows how stupid the direct attack can be. Smart adversaries change the rules. The Japanese—old masters in judo—know all about indirect combat.

Take, for example, Canon's entry into the copier business. The key strategic decision makers at Canon had a specific vision, formulated after they had spent time analyzing their major adversary. They knew that they had no chance of tackling a giant such as Xerox head on, so they went sideways; they changed the rules. Instead of offering a wide range of machines, they went for a limited number of standardized products. Instead of having a large national sales force doing their selling for them, they used office product dealers. Instead of having a national service network, they built reliability and serviceability into their products. Moreover, they sold their products; they didn't lease them, as Xerox did. Finally, buying a Canon machine was far simpler than dealing with Xerox, where heads of corporate duplication departments in each customer organization had to get involved. In dealing with Canon, department managers or secretaries handled the transaction.

Where do vision and a sense of mission come from? What happens in the intrapsychic theater of the leader, and to what extent is the leader's inner theater acted out on the public stage? Did the first Henry Ford want to make cheap cars for the farmer in order to redeem himself in the eyes of his own father, who was a farmer? How much did Walt Disney's urge to make people happy have to do with his own unhappiness as a child? And what about Steven Jobs, the former chairman of Apple who wanted to challenge IBM and change the way people work by putting a computer in every home? There are deeply rooted reasons why each of these individuals—and every other leader—has a particular outlook.

Another factor that differentiates leaders from ordinary mortals is their ability to empower people. Leaders know how to take advantage of the Pygmalion effect in management. They know how to get the best out of their people.

But how *do* you empower people? The answer is very simple. If you express high performance expectations, show that you have confidence in your employees' ability to meet those expectations, and create a facilitative structure, in most instances employees will do their utmost to oblige. This is the obvious way to build commitment. By empowering people, you enhance their self-esteem and feelings of self-confidence, often leading them to perform beyond expectations. Catherine the Great already seemed to be familiar with the Pygmalion effect in business. Wasn't it she who said, "Praise loudly, blame softly"? And Napoleon declared that every French soldier carried a marshal's baton in his knapsack. Unfortunately, this process of empowering can also work the other way: if you tell people regularly that they are idiots, they may start behaving accordingly.

The art of leadership is to create the kind of environment where people have peak experiences, where in their excitement, they become completely involved in what they are doing and lose their sense of time. And to enable that to happen, leaders need to give them a sense of control, a feeling of ownership in what they are doing. As General Patton used to say, "If you tell people where to go, but not how to get there, you'll be amazed at the results."

Another key word in describing successful leaders is *energize*. In every organization, there is an enormous amount of free-floating aggressive and affectionate energy. The art of leadership is to channel these quantities of energy in the right direction. Aggressive energy has to be directed externally; people in the organization should fight not each other but the competition. As Jack Welch of General Electric used to say, "I don't want you to fight your neighbor at the next desk. If you are in plastics, I want you to fight Du Pont; if in electronics, I want you to fight Westinghouse."

The other part of the energy management process is to use affectionate energy in an appropriate way. Every leader, at whatever level, is to some extent a kind of psychiatric social worker, a "container" of the emotions of subordinates. The way people go about creating this kind of holding environment distinguishes effective from ineffective leaders. After all, the derailment of a CEO is seldom caused by a lack of information about the latest techniques in marketing, finance, or production; rather, it comes about because of a lack of interpersonal skills—a failure to get the best out of the people who possess necessary information.

Thus the acid test in this whole process is whether you manage to get your people behind you. Others have to share your vision. If you are unable to win the support of your followers, you might as well pack up. I remember very clearly one of my leadership seminars, in which a participant told the president of a company in no uncertain terms (after having listened for some time to what the other described as his major problem), "You're a racehorse. You're running all out, but you never look back to see whether anybody is following you!" Yet without followers, there is simply no leadership.

Although I have concentrated on the charismatic side of leadership, I do not mean to exclude the instrumental role, which is also important. Designing, structuring, controlling, and rewarding are all parts of the same package. Leaders have to be organizational architects. They have to create the kind of designs and structures that facilitate the envisioning, empowering, and energizing processes of leadership. Should the company be centralized or decentralized? Should the structure be tall or flat?

Similarly, leaders have to set up the kind of control and reward systems that make enactment of the charismatic role easy. Obviously, elaborate policing systems are not going to foster empowerment. The same is true of reward systems. For example, profit-sharing systems and stock option plans give executives more of a sense of ownership. An organizational design that minimizes bureaucracy and political infighting, offers a fair reward system, and allows room for contrarian thinking will go a long way toward effective organizational functioning.

Through structuring, controlling, and rewarding, the whole charismatic aspect of leadership becomes both more concrete and more focused. Thus both roles have to be seen in their totality. One role without the other is going to be ineffective. The charismatic role combined with the instrumental role, however, makes for a very powerful package.

So after considering leadership in this way, is it still necessary to make the manager the new scapegoat of the business world? Not really fair, is it? It is clear that it is hard to be an effective leader without possessing certain managerial traits. And to be a glorious leader is not for everyone. After all, we cannot have the sort of army where everyone is a general. We also need people who do concrete things.

Today's preoccupation with leadership should be looked at as a sign of the times, a reflection of the need to have a beacon in an era of change. But it does not mean that we should throw out the baby with the bathwater and forget how to manage!

2

Welcome to the Snake Pit
The New CEO

Heroing is one of the shortest-lived professions there is.
Will Rogers

*The thing is, you see, that the strongest man in the
world is the man who stands most alone.*

Henrik Ibsen

So you have fallen for the sweet talk of the headhunter. You have
taken the plunge. You have left your safe position at your old
company and are moving to another one. You have reached the goal
you set yourself when you started out on your career: you have
finally been asked to run the show. Your predecessor in the new firm,
in spite of his psychological *Sturm und Drang*, has decided (or has
been forced) to let go. You are going to be in charge. It is exciting
but, admit it, also a bit scary. What are you going to do next? What
are your first moves going to be? What is uppermost in your mind?
What now?

First, it needs to be emphasized that there is a difference between
taking up the top job as an insider and entering as an outsider. Each
form of promotion is accompanied by special problems. The challenge faced by the new leader of an organization very much depends
on what the concerned stakeholders (shareholders, members of the
board of directors, banks, suppliers, and so on) want from him or

her. The usual working hypothesis is that if you want evolution, you take an insider; if you want revolution, you bring in an outsider.

If they choose an insider, the decision makers in a company are more or less signaling that they have chosen a maintenance strategy and do not want to rock the boat too much. The prevailing feeling will likely be that the company has been on the right course and that there is no need to make great changes. By contrast, bringing in an outsider usually indicates that decision makers are looking for someone with turnaround skills.

It is clear that an outsider is much freer than an insider to act tough. It is easier for an outsider to take on the role of hatchet wielder. He or she, unbound by long-standing social obligations and emotional ties, will be much less sentimental. An outsider can act in a much more unrestrained way, should a change in policy be needed.

But coming in as an outsider is not without its own problems. Compared to an insider, an outsider has greater difficulty in understanding how to deal with internal power structures. He or she is at a disadvantage when it comes to in-depth knowledge of the task at hand and will not yet really understand what is needed to be successful in the new role. The outsider has to get to know the people, understand the organizational processes and procedures, and build up contacts. (Of course, executives who have been in a similar position in a firm operating in a comparable industry may feel less at a disadvantage than someone taking on a new role in a completely new environment.)

So what should you do if you come in as an outsider? What should your first steps be? What pitfalls should you look out for?

Take, for example, the case of Louis Gerstner, former chairman of RJR Nabisco, who took over as CEO of IBM. Obviously, the board had lost confidence in his predecessor, John Akers, and had become both impatient with the rate of change at IBM and concerned about the company's continuing financial hemorrhage. Board members probably felt that to expedite the turnaround process, an outsider had to be brought in. Interestingly enough, they brought in an outsider from a very different industry, despite the fact that an outsider who knows the industry tends to more effective in such an instance. Coming in as an outsider both to the company and the industry is a real challenge!

A *Fortune* article described what preoccupied Gerstner during his first thirty days on the job. Understandably, the first thing he did was to talk to the top management group, asking John Akers to make the introductions. When questioned about how he spent his time during that first month, he said that mostly he just listened to people, roamed all over the company, and read E-mail notes.

Gerstner did change a few things quickly, however. For example, he was very impatient with the rather formal way of reporting at IBM—through presentations accompanied by zillions of transparencies. He asked his executives to find a more spontaneous way of reporting (and they did). Another thing high on his list was discovering as quickly as possible the company's competitive position. This information was needed to help him formulate a set of new business objectives.

From the comments in the article, it is clear that Gerstner began by making a number of generalized statements (after all, he was still trying to figure out the workings of the company) about such things as the need to be more customer- and market-driven and the necessity to organize the company in such a way that it would be as effective as possible with a minimum of bureaucracy.[1] Soon after his interview with *Fortune,* however, he went one step further and moved to overhaul IBM's existing 40,000-strong U.S. marketing force. Instead of organizing the sales staff by geographical region and having salespeople sell everything from PCs to mainframes, he created a focus on product and industry specialties. To be more customer-responsive, the sales force is now divided in such a way that specialists familiar with specific industries and computer products do the selling within their specialty, as opposed to everyone selling everything.

This Gerstner example gives an idea of what the new CEO is up against. It says something about the things he or she has to find out, the questions that have to be asked. In the first place, it is helpful to know what your initial mandate is going to be. What is the nature of your assignment? What do the people who brought you into the organization expect from you? Have they hired you because you possess a particular skill? Is it because you are good at cutting costs? Do they want you because of your creative abilities? Are you one of those rare global executives who can give the company a more international focus? Do you have any specific functional skills (production, marketing, financial, or legal) that will come in handy? The answers to these questions will be vitally important in determining your initial mandate.

Furthermore, the situation you face upon entry will be quite different if you are dealing with a successful corporation as opposed to one that is in trouble. Bringing in an outsider is usually symptomatic of the latter situation, however. In that case, a clear break from the previous regime may be what is wanted. In the former situation, it is generally much harder to implement major changes.

Returning to the question of how to manage the entry process, it is imperative to spend some time with the members of the board of directors at the outset. It is also extremely useful (if possible) to have some contact with your predecessor. Of course, this will depend on the terms under which the latter is leaving. Is it a natural departure, or is it a forced one? (As a matter of fact, I hope you had some frank discussions with these people *before* you took the plunge, to counteract the seductive talk of the headhunter who solicited you.) Among the questions to consider are these: What does your predecessor see as the major problems in the company? Do the board members think the same? What do they have to say about the performance of the person you are succeeding? Why have they chosen you? What do they want you to do?

It is in your own best interest to build some kind of coalition with board members. Failure to do so can be very costly. The most critical function of the board, of course, is to select, assess, reward, and replace CEOs. Do not brush this fact aside. CEOs can be replaced. Estimates vary, but an educated guess indicates that 10 percent of all newly appointed CEOs get fired.[2] A further 5 percent fail within the first three years. You had better take steps to ensure that you do not become a member of this group of losers.

Another important part of the board's mandate is the setting of direction. I am not talking about operational decisions here, but about major strategic reorientations. Last but certainly not least, it is also the board's duty to safeguard the ethical and legal conduct of the organization and its members.

As a caveat, it should be mentioned that effecting dramatic change is much more difficult if there is a tradition, as there is in many companies, of making the outgoing CEO a member of the board. If that is the case, the ex-CEO may interpret change as an indictment of his or her tenure and make efforts to resist it. Thus you would be well advised to ascertain what the prospective company's practice is before you commit yourself to any new assignment.

So, having come in as the new CEO, how much time do you have before you have to take action? Should you wait a while or start acting immediately? Some people argue (depending, of course, on the urgency of the situation) that, like incoming U.S. presidents, new CEOs should have the famous ninety days to prove their mettle. More precisely, these ninety days can be divided into two periods: a listening stage (of thirty days) and a testing stage (sixty days). During the first three months of your tenure, you assess obstacles and test options, in order to be ready to take action in the subsequent implementation stage.

As far as your anxiety about the right way to approach your new job is concerned, you should remember that you are not alone. Think about how the other people in the company feel. They will be apprehensive about having a newcomer in charge. They will ask themselves what you are going to change and what you will leave alone; what you are like as a person; whether they will be able to live with you; whether you will respect the existing culture; whether you will want to change the course of the company. They will be scared about their own jobs. You are anxious; they are anxious—there's lots of anxiety floating around. This emotional problem has to be addressed.

One common but dangerous response of newcomers to corporate situations that are anxiety-ridden is known as flight into action. Action is a typical human response to anxiety, after all. But it is particularly dangerous, since in stressful situations we have a tendency to regress, falling back into patterns of behavior that we have previously been comfortable with. These actions may be related to areas of our particular expertise, to be sure, but these areas may not be those where action is most needed. To act without really knowing what has to be done is not the wisest of strategies, and having to backtrack later is not very good for building confidence among the executive group. (Of course, backtracking is better than just digging in and compounding a bad decision.)

One executive I know who has built a considerable reputation as a turnaround manager once told me his recipe for success. His action plan is quite simple and certainly does not take ninety days. He believes in shortening the agony, asserting that changes should not be dragged out. He comes in to his new company like Attila the Hun, starting off by firing the whole second management layer. He then replaces half the people he has just fired with executives from the third layer, reasoning that this promoted group of executives will feel indebted and that the promotions will show all executives in the company that there are possibilities for upward mobility. He then replaces the other half of the second layer with outsiders (not surprisingly, some from his previous companies); in his opinion, this is the best way to ensure loyalty.

This may be a very dramatic way of going about things, but in certain situations, a newcomer does not have much of a choice. If you are really there to instigate a revolution, you may *have* to reach down to the third layer: people at the second layer may well have become too set in their ways. You have to build alliances with potential change-makers within the company.

Of course, this is a very draconian way of achieving change. There are other ways of going about it. The following technique has often proved successful. Upon arrival, after making some very general preliminary comments (perhaps saying something about one's previous background and yet remaining unspecific about plans), the newcomer should just walk around the company and listen—and I mean *really* listen. The trick is to obtain as much information as possible in the shortest possible time.

The newcomer should not rely simply on internal information in this process but should talk also to customers and suppliers. What do they say about the company? What do they like about it? What are their complaints? It is important to have their collaboration. Customer and supplier relations tell a lot about the internal workings of the company. Bankers and consultants can also be extremely useful sources of information. This information gathering has been part of Gerstner's approach at IBM.

The next vital thing for the newcomer is to select key collaborators—the people who are going to help him or her put plans into action. Who is going to be on the team, and who is not? Are there people whose loyalty is questionable? These things have to be discovered quickly; and to do this, the newcomer has to be able to rely on interpersonal skills.

The first impression you make in the company is going to be extremely important. Remember that people will be watching you very closely. The rumor mill will be working overtime. Are you supportive? Do you respect other people's opinions? Do you practice what you preach? Are you credible? It is essential at this point to gain the trust of the people you want to work with. You have to build coalitions and sort out working relationships.

What makes this process so difficult is that you may have to get rid of the people who thought that they were going to get your job and who may now be preparing to sabotage your tenure. The last thing you need is to have a bunch of wounded Hamlets lurking about!

Having gathered information and aligned a group of collaborators, you next have to confront what is in many ways a chicken-and-egg issue: you have to articulate a vision and a strategic mandate. When people have some kind of direction, they have a roadmap; they have something to hold on to, something on which a realistic set of performance expectations can be erected. That direction decreases the existing free-floating anxiety. However, you may not yet know enough about the company to be very specific. Meanwhile, your time, particularly in situations of crisis, is quite limited. That being the case, the best thing to do (and here you may be helped by the members of the board, who with luck have been very clear about their expectations) is to set some simple, general initial goals. You can fine-tune them later. To make sure that everyone understands, you should repeat these goals loud and clear, over and over again. People have to be continually reminded of them.

You will also have to recognize and learn how to deal with some of the psychological dimensions affecting you and the company. As a newcomer, people may well look up to you as the long-awaited messiah, particularly if things have not been going well in the organization. If things were going badly before your arrival, you will be supposed to set them right. You will be regarded, at the outset, as the new hero. However, let me remind you that heroes tend to have a very temporary existence. People do not have much patience with them. Heroes who fail to deliver quickly may very well be vilified and end up as scapegoats. In the hero-worship business, emotional attachments can be very fickle.

The actress Ingrid Bergman once said that happiness is good health and a bad memory. The same thing applies to the way people behave in organizational life. There is such a thing as the Rebecca myth in organizations—a tendency to romanticize the past. Daphne du Maurier's novel *Rebecca* is the story of a young woman who marries a widower and is haunted by people's idealized memory of his first wife, whose apparent virtues are continually extolled. All the negative things about her initially seem to have been forgotten. Likewise, within organizations the previous regime—however bad it may have been—quickly becomes idealized. If newcomers do not deliver the goods quickly, the same process may start to operate against them. Before they know it, everything they do will be seen in a negative light, in spite of many actions taken for the better.

After all this, are you still interested in the top job? Or do you feel that there are better things to do in life? Obviously, coming in as a new CEO can be risky. Mistakes will be made. But life is not a rehearsal. Only those who do nothing will make no mistakes. Change is stressful, but it may also make you feel more alive. And taking over the top job is only the beginning. As we shall see in the following essays, change is one of the major themes in organizational life.

. . . .

3

Boiled Frogs and Dancing Elephants
Change and Downsizing

Chaos often breeds life, while order breeds habit.
Henry Adams

That horse whose rider fears to jump will fall,
Riflemen miss if orders sound unsure;
They only are secure who seem secure;
Who lose their voice, lose all.
Kingsley Amis

Change does not come easily. As Woodrow Wilson once said, "If you want to make enemies, try to change something." Change invites resistance on many different levels—individual, cultural, and organizational. The real problem is that people do not like being changed. They do not like things being done to them. They have a more positive attitude toward change, however, if they can initiate the change process themselves. Unfortunately, this happens all too rarely.

When was the last time you did a biology experiment? Probably longer ago than you care to remember. Why not try again? Take a pot of hot water and a frog. Throw the frog into the pot. What do you think will happen? The obvious, of course: the frog will jump out. Who likes hanging around in a pot of hot water? Now try something else. Take a pot of cold water, put the frog in it, and place the pot on the stove. Turn on the heat. This time something different will occur. The frog, because of the incremental change in temperature, will not notice that it is slowly being boiled.

Unfortunately, many organizations, as they grow, begin to resemble the boiled frog. The graveyard of business is littered with companies that failed to recognize inevitable changes taking place around them. Companies tend to become complacent; they stop paying attention to changing market conditions and shifting customer needs. They are all too often lulled to sleep by past successes.

Far too many executives have discovered too late that nothing kills like success. Success encourages complacency in organizations. It is unlikely to stimulate organizational learning, and an absence of learning can be fatal. "We learn little from success but much from failure," according to an Arab proverb. But it is not only complacency that inhibits learning; another reason people stop learning is that, having experienced success, they are less willing to risk failure. It is quite correct to say that people who never try never fail. Organizations that lose the will to try become more and more lethargic. They begin to resemble something large and lumbering: an elephant, perhaps?

What can be done about this? How can organizations avoid slipping into complacency? How can they be made to change? How can we get an elephant to dance?

In many instances, change that is imposed on people unleashes a multitude of fears: of the unknown, of loss of freedom, of loss of status or position, of loss of authority and responsibility, and of loss of good working conditions and money. These fears may be most acute at the top of an organization, where power equations play a role; change may be interpreted at this level as an indictment of the existing leadership, with the threat of redistribution of power. One result is creativity-stifling attitudes such as, "Someone else has already tried what you're suggesting, and it didn't work," or "We've invested too much money in this project. We can't change in midstream."

Change is never painless. In fact, pain is frequently the prime motivator that sets the change process into motion: *pathemata mathemata*, "learn by suffering," as the ancient Greeks said. Unfortunately, I have rarely met a person willing to change when things are going well. Likewise, there are very few organizations that engage in change as a kind of preventive maintenance, that attempt to detect when the water is coming to a boil. Usually, some kind of catastrophe is needed before they start to react. Continuous change, however, is an inevitable part of human existence. Without the capacity to adapt, the organism will die. As Heraclitus said, "There is nothing permanent in life except change."

What people often fail to take into account is that change necessitates a type of mourning process. People have to mourn the things they are leaving behind. The feelings prompted by significant change can be compared to what children experience when their mothers leave them. This mourning process—our familiar pattern of dealing with stressful experiences—begins in childhood and is repeated throughout life.

Change thus implies some form of loss. When this loss occurs, it is usually followed by a number of distinct stages. The first of these is a phase of disarray, in which the individuals affected may have a sense of numbness, interrupted by feelings of panic and outbursts of anger. This phase is inevitable; one has to go through it. Any attempt to divert it only causes greater problems. The feelings associated with the loss will then pop up later, often with a much more devastating effect.

This phase is usually followed by a period of yearning and searching for what is lost, which may be accompanied by feelings of disbelief and denial of the new reality. Executives facing change in their organization may assume a reactive position and try to hang on to the past, showing no concern for the future. They may experience bouts of self-reproach and sadness.

However, if people are allowed to work through the mourning process, this state of discontent will be followed by a discarding of the patterns of thinking, feeling, and acting of the past. There will be greater acceptance of the new situation, both personally and organizationally; there will be a willingness to go through a process of self-examination and a redefinition of oneself. Tentative explorations will be made toward establishing a new equilibrium.

In the final stage of the change process, the person's internal psychic world is redefined. There is a sense of hope; new choices seem possible. There is also a more proactive attitude and an orientation toward the future. This phase marks the fact that the executives in the organization have come to grips with the new reality.

One organization that has successfully undergone a traumatic change is Zeiss Jena, once a flagship of East German industry. In 1989, before the borders opened, Zeiss Jena was the center of a *Kombinat*—a large conglomerate of diverse industries that had grown up over time and employed more than 70,000 people. Its original brief—to manufacture precision optical, mechanical, and electronic instruments—had expanded over the years to include micro-electronics and cameras. Its most important customer was the USSR, whose rockets and satellite stations were chock-full of equipment made in Jena.

At Zeiss, subcontracting was unknown. The organization produced everything itself, from the tiniest screw to the finished product. The East German government knew that for any difficult industrial assignment, one could always call on Zeiss. People at Zeiss were miracle workers, the crème de la crème; they could make anything. Western import restrictions, however, had forced Zeiss into certain industries (such as computers) that, given the economics of the marketplace, it had no business being in. The close interchange between people at Zeiss and the Friedrich Schiller University made Jena the heart of the military-industrial complex of East Germany.

Then calamity struck, at least for Zeiss Jena: the Berlin Wall came down. The high-priced West German Mark became the new currency. Suddenly, many of the products for which, before November 1989, the company had had trouble meeting demand became less attractive to purchasers. Zeiss's fledgling adventures in micro-electronics collapsed. The company had no hope of competing with the West in that field. It was much the same for Zeiss's camera industry: Japanese cameras were not only cheaper but also much better. So much for large chunks of the *Kombinat*. As many businesses in the West were finding, it was time to turn back to the original core activities.

What do you do when your whole Eastern European market is in shambles? What do you do when a major part of your market, which was especially aimed at military production, no longer exists? What do you do when your products are no longer competitive? What do you do when you have no idea what your products cost and where you make your profits? How do you institute an attitudinal change among your executives, going from a command economy to a market economy, making clear that your products will no longer automatically be sold? (This last revolution, a revolution in the mind, remains the most difficult one to handle.)

All this has to be seen in the context of an infrastructure that was on the verge of collapse even before the change in outlook for Zeiss Jena became necessary. Although the German government is investing massive amounts of money to change the situation, it will take time before communications, services, and conditions improve in the former East Germany. The roads (many now under reconstruction) are terrible. The telephone service is being completely overhauled. Living standards are improving only slowly, and environmental conditions are abysmal (due to an exceptionally high level of pollution).

One of the most dramatic responses Zeiss Jena made to all these economic and political changes was an almost incredible number of job cuts. From a 1989 figure of 70,000, the labor force shrank initially to 27,000, reaching a final figure of 3,000 employees (although that figure depends on the way one calculates the split of the company into two major parts—more on that later).

If this were not problem enough, the company's executive group had simultaneously to go through a kind of purification effort. A task force dealing with executive selection was put into operation, and for several years every senior job in the company was up for grabs. The mandate of the task force was to review all positions in the three top layers of management and decide on the competence of the various candidates. An important part of the agenda was to detect any skeletons hanging in the cupboards of executives, meaning Stasi or party connections. Although such a task force may have been necessary, its presence did not add to the peace of mind of an already highly stressed group of executives.

There was another complicated problem to be tackled as well. There is not one Zeiss, but two. Apart from the Zeiss in Jena, there is also one—a younger sibling—in Oberkochen, West Germany. In fact, Zeiss represents a remarkable story of a company's survival against all odds. It demonstrates the strength of the glue that kept the company together: a corporate culture that made the Zeissianer determined not to let their company die.

It all started at the end of the Second World War. The Americans were the first of the Allies to arrive in Jena, and they recognized a good thing when they saw one. Off to America went patents, documentation, construction machinery, and the best scientists, many of whom stayed in the United States permanently. Three days later, the Russians arrived. Their visit took care of the remaining scientists and machinery. Stalin had the whole caboodle shipped off to Leningrad.

You might think this would finish off any company. Not Zeiss. There was still life left in it. Some of the scientists and technicians who had made it to the West decided to start anew, and in Oberkochen they found a place that resembled the ambience they had left behind in Jena. However, the company's remarkable ability to survive was not confined to the West. In Jena itself, even after this dramatic dismantling of the entire company, the spirit of Zeiss lived on. From 1949 on, the remaining Zeissianer began the reconstruction of their company in their hometown.

As might be expected, Zeiss Jena and Zeiss Oberkochen became fierce competitors, each claiming the exclusive right to the famous brand name. So, apart from an already formidable clutch of problems by the time of German reunification, management in Jena also had to worry about the implications of a possible reunification with Zeiss Oberkochen. Given its state of internal chaos, and its distorted product portfolio, Zeiss Jena was in a terrible bargaining position.

The onerous task of playing Solomon in this situation was assigned to the *Treuhandanstalt* in Berlin, the government agency charged with the privatization effort in the former East Germany. This agency worked in consultation with the government of Thüringen (the state in which Jena is located) and Zeiss Oberkochen.

Finding a solution to the Zeiss affair was not easy. There were enormous pressures on all the stakeholders. Because of the gigantic scale of layoffs, peace within the workforce was seriously threatened. The Zeissianer were anything but happy as the process began, as a number of large demonstrations showed at the time. The murder in Berlin of the president of the *Treuhandanstalt* added to the climate of unrest.

When I visited Jena some years ago—after the Wall had fallen but before Zeiss had rebuilt itself—the television cameras, the barbed wire, and the armed guards were already gone. I had no difficulty getting into the sanctum sanctorum—the center of Zeiss Jena's research and development. The monstrous Stalinist buildings were almost empty. The executives and scientists who still remained appeared shellshocked, wondering where to go from here—how to commercialize the outcome of their research.

At the time, I asked myself, "What on earth can be done here?" Those who had followed the history of Zeiss might well have said, "Plus ça change, plus c'est la même chose." By now, Zeissianer should be specialists in pulling themselves up by their bootstraps, they would argue. With its history, Zeiss should know how to deal with business cycles. After all, the dramatic disassembly of the company after the Second World War (during which it had been geared up for war production) was not the first time Zeiss had faced a reverse in its fortunes. The period after the First World War was not without turmoil of its own. That was also a time of drastic downsizing: the workforce was reduced from 50,000 to 7,000 people.

Although Zeiss Jena may have learned something from the past, this time the Zeissianer have to demonstrate just how good they are at economic acrobatics. The chosen solution has been a partial integration with Zeiss Oberkochen (streamlining their product lines) and the creation of a separate company called Jenoptik, whose main business will be to create high-tech spin-offs to keep Jena on the map as a technological center of excellence.

The people who have been asked to stop the intellectual hemorrhage at Zeiss have been up against extraordinary odds. How does one cope with this type of discontinuity? How does one go about downsizing and still maintain morale in an organization? This is not a problem only for Zeiss Jena, of course. Retrenchment is an issue many senior executives are currently struggling with. Downsizing has become a reality in many countries.

What is the best way to lay people off? Through attrition? Through early retirement encouraged by golden handshakes? What if the corporation is losing huge sums of money? In that case, the amount involved in golden handshakes might endanger the survival of the whole company. Should people be let go immediately, or should they be allowed time to adjust? After the years they have invested in the company, would it not be fair to give them a chance to work through the bad news, to mourn their losses? On the other hand, having these dismissed people around is bound to affect morale. The inevitable side effects of downsizing are anger, grief, and a loss of self-esteem. Managing this emotional fallout is difficult and painful and may have to be done case by case. This will mean additional stress and further demands on already overstretched resources of time and energy.

Whatever the organization decides to do, it is wise to be as decent as possible about the way you let people go. Even at Zeiss, an extreme example of downsizing, a serious attempt was made to make people aware of why changes were happening. There is always an obligation to keep people informed; if you fail to, various forms of paranoia may emerge. And paranoid thinking carries a heavy price in terms of human misery.

At Zeiss, enormous efforts were made to keep employees employed at least part-time. Because that was not always possible, employees were given the opportunity to start spin-off operations and to participate in retraining programs. The people in charge of the company made a valiant attempt to keep the workers informed of developments. In spite of that, a certain amount of paranoid thinking could not be avoided, and some of the most capable employees—people top management had hoped would stay on— left for jobs with companies in West Germany.

What is of key importance in these painful situations is that employees should at least have a sense of fairness about the whole process, difficult as it might be. Remember that the people who stay will pay close attention to the way in which those who are laid off are treated. With corporate loyalty in danger of flying out the window, conspicuously fair treatment for laid-off staff is a very good long-term investment.

Failure to handle downsizing decently will alienate employees and cause a breakdown in creative and effective team spirit at a time when it is most needed. Performance is inevitably affected in such situations. Any adverse publicity will also affect relationships with other stakeholders, such as bankers and suppliers. It may be a good idea to bring in outplacement consultants to facilitate the transition process, minimize the pain, and help the dismissed people find other jobs.

But what reactions can we observe among the survivors of downsizing? Unfortunately, one of the most immediate results is the development of an us-versus-them attitude. All of a sudden, people begin to ostracize employees who are to be let go, perhaps believing that they are to be blamed for the mess in which the company finds itself. Scapegoating is a very natural, if unhelpful, response to a miserable situation. One interpretation of such behavior is that it is a way of managing a bad conscience. However, this is a dysfunctional way of dealing with survivor guilt. Predictably, these reactions were occasionally observed at Zeiss, where some of the more obviously employable employees could be seen to withdraw from people who were once very close colleagues.

Deciding where to apportion blame for the misfortunes of the company can be a very tricky business. Are top executives going to assume full responsibility? Are unrealistic union demands to blame? Can external reasons be found? If it is possible to find an external cause, anger can be directed toward a visible outside scapegoat. This tends to be a more positive way of metabolizing aggressive feelings. Of course, Zeiss was a very special case. Here the major causes were German reunification, the fall of Communism, and the ill-conceived currency union. Nevertheless, top management did not entirely escape the wrath of many employees.[1] In other companies, the reasons are more directly company-based, such as management decisions that have been poorly thought through. For example, the faulty strategic decision of John Akers, former president of IBM, to bet on large mainframe computers instead of the much smaller PCs, is largely responsible for present redundancies at the company.

Communication is a key factor in managing the downsizing process. Explaining the reasons for downsizing is not enough, however. The remaining employees also need to be told what the new strategy is going to be. Receiving only painful news leads employees to depressive thoughts. There should be hope for a new future as well. There should be an understanding of what the process of retrenchment implies. Involving employees in the process will reduce feelings of helplessness. It must be clear to employees that the changes are being made because of new realities in the marketplace. Retrenchment should be presented as a challenge, as a way to create a greater level of effectiveness and efficiency in the operation, as a way to reinvent the corporation. This is exactly what IBM, under Louis Gerstner's new leadership, is now doing. The remaining executives have been given an opportunity to rebuild what was once one of the world's most exciting corporations.

Remember also that downsizing feeds the rumor mill. Because false rumors spread like wildfire, the potential for paranoid thinking should never be underestimated. The rumor damage can be limited by a flow of accurate information, however; a clear view of the new direction in which the company is headed will help the remaining executives to concentrate on the business at hand. For the duration of the downsizing process, and for a lengthy period afterward, as much information should be disclosed as possible. This is definitely not a time to stay silent. Even if an executive does not know why certain events are taking place, it is better to be honest and say so.

Bear in mind that it is not enough to offer financial incentives to the remaining star executives. Without the hope of a better future, and a vision of their critical role in it, these people are not going to hang around. Since the psychological contract between each person and the organization has been disrupted, a sense of trust has to be reestablished.

One company I know of mismanaged the process of downsizing by making false promises, giving misinformation, and treating the dismissed executives in a rather callous manner. This way of acting was combined with an attempt to dangle positions of increased responsibility and income in front of some of the potential high fly-ers who had been asked to stay with the company. The ploy failed, however, as these executives quickly became fed up with the way things were managed. Most of them left the company voluntarily to join some of the executives dismissed in the downsizing exercise in a new venture in the same industry. Because of the loss of criti-cal personnel and the emergence of an aggressive new competitor, the original company had to file for bankruptcy within two years.

There are no easy answers to the problem of downsizing. It is one of the most difficult and painful challenges that executives have to deal with. Management at Zeiss faced an extremely distressing and stressful task, but at least the drastic measures taken seem to be producing results: the new Zeiss is on its way.

It is not easy to act as catalyst for such change processes. Ani-mating a lethargic organization requires a lot of drive and energy, along with a large dose of political savvy. One person who has man-aged to bring new life to an organizational elephant is Jack Welch, the chairman of General Electric. When he took over from his predecessor, Reginald Jones, in 1981, the company had become increasingly bureaucratic. It was suffering from organizational arteriosclerosis: the bureaucracy effect. Executives were drowning in paper.

How can you change a company as big as General Electric? Welch knew that you cannot make an omelet without breaking eggs, and he planned to make a gigantic omelet. As a result, many General Electric executives had to go through the kind of mourning process described earlier. What helped them, however, was that Welch did not only inflict pain; he had a vision of the future, an idea of where he wanted to go, and he recognized the importance of transmitting that vision to the people in his organization. He knew that merely cutting costs by laying people off would not be enough.

Welch started by spreading a simple message throughout the corporation. He stated that divisions that were not already number one or number two in their particular business had better try to get there fast; and if they needed additional resources, they should ask for them. If they failed to make the grade, they would be "disengaged"—Welch's euphemism for being sacked. Welch was not nicknamed "Neutron Jack" for nothing. The bittersweet joke at GE was that after each of Welch's visits to one of his facilities, the building would be left standing, but a lot of corpses would be lying around. Year after year, Welch ranked number one on *Fortune* magazine's list of the toughest executives in North America. He meant business. He started out by disengaging a quarter of the workforce at General Electric: he sold some 200 businesses and closed 73 plants and facilities, a total reduction of about 100,000 employees. But he also acquired businesses in areas where he felt General Electric could be successful.

A new disease spread through the company: "Welchitis," a virus originating with Welch that was supposed to change the corporate culture. Welch was not particularly subtle in the way he put his message across. He has always been a strong believer in constructive conflict. He argues and yells when he feels like it, at times letting his street-fighter background get the better of him. The people he respects most are the ones who stand their ground and fight back. His way of thinking is probably best understood in terms of a game of ice hockey: you push and shove your opponent for the duration of the match, but after the game is over, you go and have a beer together.

Welch's specialty when he started his program of change at GE was "delayering"—cutting layers of extraneous fat out of the corporation. Traditional concepts of span of control and hierarchy seem to be meaningless to him. Welch likes to create constant turmoil and talks about the organization without boundaries. He is also a strong believer in the overworked manager engaging in company "workouts." Here company "rattlesnakes"—factors that hamper progress and cause conflict (problems to do with meetings, reports, procedures, or approval or measurement systems)—are killed on the spot. Executives make personal commitments to reorganize work and maximize returns on time spent working in the organization.

Welch wants people in the organization who are entrepreneurial, who possess a sense of ownership about what they are doing. He wants people who act. In his company, people who stand in the middle of the road and do nothing are sure to be run over. He is very aware of the fact that organizational design and speed have become competitive advantages in our global world.

Welch may be abrasive and unorthodox, but he has been extremely successful in accomplishing what he set out to do. General Electric has achieved market-share leadership in nearly all of its fourteen businesses. The transformation has been a traumatic experience, however, for members of the old core businesses, loyalty having become, it could be said, only twenty-four hours deep. T-shirts that read "Subscribe to Jack's values or else . . ." say a fair bit about the atmosphere in the company when disengagement was at its peak.

Jack Welch is nobody's fool, however. He realizes that in order to change a corporate culture, he has to build in a period of consolidation after the period of reanimation. To enable that process to happen, he has taken the route of management development. He is a regular visitor at the company's training center in Crotonville. In spite of his busy schedule—running a $60 billion empire requires a great deal of energy—he is present at almost every senior executive program to clarify and argue his philosophy.[2]

The question is whether other giants, such as Philips, IBM, and General Motors, are capable of taking up the same challenge and becoming as competitive. Are these elephants that can be made to dance, or will they suffer the ignoble end of the boiled frog?

The days are long gone when the statement "What is good for General Motors is good for America," uttered by a former president of General Motors, had any relevance. Recently, General Motors went through a kind of palace revolution executed by impatient external board members who had become fed up with the snail-like pace of change in the company. The same can be said about other large firms.

The need for change can be observed in many companies in other countries as well. The giant electronics firm Philips, under its latest CEO, Jan Timmer, is now engaged in "Operation Centurion" to increase competitiveness. This company suffered not only from organizational arteriosclerosis but also from what might be called the Mr. Magoo effect. Mr. Magoo was an incredibly shortsighted cartoon character who constantly misinterpreted what was going on around him. Self-delusion, symptoms of the not-invented-here syndrome, unwillingness to face and deal with bad news, and overoptimism are not unusual in many of these companies.

We have seen that maintaining excellence is never easy. But in the end, do you really have a choice? Inaction may be fatal. If you maintain a passive stance, the boiled frog phenomenon can prove deadly. It would be better, perhaps, to be inspired by an earlier stage in the frog's life cycle: its metamorphosis from a tadpole! In fact, it is often a recognition of the need to grow and adapt that motivates organizations to undergo a similar process: that of mergers and acquisitions.

4

Merger Fever
Managing Acquisition

Alliance, n. *In international politics, the union of two thieves who have their hands so deeply inserted in each other's pocket that they cannot separately plunder a third.*

Ambrose Bierce

The big-business mergers and the big-labor mergers have all the appearances of dinosaurs mating.

John Naisbitt

Some companies get smaller; others get bigger. Of course, most people who have a choice will opt for growth. One way of getting there is through mergers and acquisitions. The merger epidemic is not as recent a phenomenon as one might think. After the frenzy of the 1980s, some observers have noted that the fever is becoming less virulent. That does not mean, however, that it has stopped spreading. On the contrary.

What is the reason for the epidemic? Why has it been spreading so rapidly? Are infected executives merely indulging their ego, or is there more to it than that?

The reasons given for mergers and acquisitions are often based on rational economic arguments. Business performance criteria, such as size and growth, economies of scale, profitability, increase in market share, and market power, are frequently cited as motives.

Taking the merger and acquisition route can supposedly help a company attain a market position at a speed that would not be possible through normal internal development. It thus becomes a new form of value creation.

A major stimulus for merger and acquisition fever has been the changing geopolitical situation. There are the competitive challenges posed by Japan, South Korea, Taiwan, and other countries of the Pacific Rim. Then there are the changes that have followed the fall of the Berlin Wall and the opening of Eastern Europe. And— even though the event has lost some of its bloom—there was 1992, a critical date signifying freedom of movement of goods, services, and people in the European Common Market. All these developments have created an enormous amount of uncertainty. With uncertainty comes anxiety. This in turn brings us to reasons for mergers and acquisitions that go beyond merely economic argument.

Executives tend to be an anxious bunch. So many things are going on over which they feel they have little control. People tend to look for some form of support when they feel anxious. A child threatened by a bully will try to create an alliance, preferably with a bigger person—a parent or an older brother. Adults who feel threatened merge, acquire, or organize a strategic partnership.

Another reason for mergers and acquisitions might be a certain amount of boredom on the part of top management. Executives who have been running the same kind of business for many years know how it works; they can get a little bit fed up with it and crave something different. What better way to cure the boredom than by becoming a modern-day Viking: raping and plundering. Takeover battles certainly get the adrenaline going. There is one key question, however, to be addressed: Will mergers and acquisitions bring the expected rewards, or will an unknown number of evils be let loose instead?

There is a certain amount of irony in this passion for growth. Just when most executives have begun to realize that salvation does not necessarily come from economies of scale—that small really is beautiful—there has been a paradoxical increase in mergers and acquisitions due to the fear of being crushed in the global game. Despite widespread agreement with Robert Townsend, the former president of Avis, who liked to say that excellence and large size are fundamentally incompatible, the growth continues.

There is often a false belief that only giants can be global players. Merger talks fill the columns of the financial pages of the newspapers. The Swiss company Brown Boveri merges with Swedish ASEA AB; the Dutch ABN bank merges with its arch competitor, the AMRO bank; and British Telecom acquires a part of MCI. Strategic alliances are formed between companies such as Renault and Mitsubishi; Big Blue lines up with German Siemens and Japanese Toshiba to develop a new generation of computers; General Motors joins forces with Toyota.

While a merger is like a marriage, a strategic alliance is more like an affair. Looking at some of these alliances, one gets the distinct impression that while initially there may have been many fantasies about the pleasures of bedding down together, the reality all too often turns out to be a cold shower. A 1993 study by McKinsey showed that one-third of the forty-nine alliances tracked did not work out.

This does not mean (to continue the metaphor) that a strategic alliance cannot end up as a stable marriage. A lot depends on the strategic significance of the partnership. But making a partnership work demands a lot of attention and commitment of resources, and one cannot expect immediate results. One should look at such an alliance as the beginning of a long-term relationship; it usually takes a lot of time and energy to know and to trust one's partner. Another important factor to remember is that strategic partnerships are new forms of competition. They can be viewed as a way of amortizing the high costs of research and product development by getting speedy access to products and markets worldwide.

Strategic alliances are inherently unstable. Trust is a delicate thing, and paranoia spreads rapidly in the wake of an alliance. To minimize paranoia, it is important to choose a partner whose products are complementary rather than competitive. There should also be a precise delineation of boundaries so that each party understands its mutual obligations and is aware of how far it can go. In the interest of balance of power, partners should treat each other as equals, even if that is not really the case.

Mergers and acquisitions are more intense relationships than alliances. Research shows that mergers have a less than 50 percent chance of being really successful. In fact, roughly one out of three acquisitions comes undone. In addition, between 50 and 75 percent of key executives in acquired companies leave voluntarily within a few years, because most people are psychologically unprepared for the aftermath of a merger or acquisition.[1]

There are a number of ways by which the process of culture integration following a merger or acquisition can be made easier. Friendly approaches naturally tend to have a more successful outcome than unfriendly ones; like all relationships, mergers and acquisitions seem to be more successful between consenting parties. Previous acquisition experience is also an advantage. Not surprisingly, companies from the same industries are likely to have a more successful union. Size also plays a role: small sellers tend to be less successful. Other obvious advantages include financial health and adequate resources on the part of both buyer and seller.

Research indicates that many mergers fail to lead to improved performance. In its May 20, 1985, issue, *Business Week* ran a cover story that posed the question, "Do mergers really work?" The answer reached in that article was no, not very often. All too frequently, the participating financial wizards, who have done their calculations and made the merger seem attractive, become victims of their own enthusiasm. With so many experts working on the merger process, it may assume a life of its own, leading to premature closure and a lot of unhappiness afterward. Financial wizards are not always perceptive about the human side of this process, yet insensitivity to the companies' varying corporate cultures can have disastrous results.

Apart from the question of cultural compatibility, which we will examine in Chapter Five, there are the issues of compatibility related to compensation, degree of autonomy, corporate objectives, and procedures. Many executives succumb to the urge to push certain procedures down the throat of the acquired company, for example. I have dealt with many newly acquired companies whose personnel were required by the corporate head office to submit information that was of no actual use to either party. The imposition of rules is often more a question of ego, the result of a determination to show who is in charge, than a move propelled by common sense or business logic.

The clash of cultures and procedures can lead to a postmerger drifting process. One indication of such a drift is the manifestation of the defensive psychological process of splitting, a phenomenon in which people always categorize others as either superior or inferior to themselves. A win-or-lose mentality may also prevail, with all the predictable power struggles. Other symptoms of drifting are job dissatisfaction, absenteeism, a high turnover of talented personnel, and decreased performance.

The lesson is obvious: do not hop on the merger bandwagon too quickly. You may lose your shirt (and very likely more) as you take it on. However, if—in spite of all the risks—you still feel like going ahead with the merger-marriage, you would do well to pay attention to some of the more elusive processes involved. Let us take a closer look.

It is very important that the top management of both companies be involved in the merger process, because merger management is critical. Top management of the acquired company should get to know the other company's management during the negotiation process in a social as well as a business context. Many choice bits of information can be picked up during social encounters. Have dinner together; meet at each other's homes!

Close investigation reveals that there is a wide gap between what senior executives say they do and what they actually practice.

Over and over again in my consulting work, when I ask CEOs to describe their management style, I am given a description of a reborn philosopher-king—only to find out quickly, by watching them interact with their subordinates, that an Attila-the-Hun style is much closer to the truth! Given these difficulties in perception, it is essential to foresee and prevent potential misunderstandings by identifying the other party's true management style and discussing in advance factors that may become problematic.

Among the many factors that can cause complications is an incompatibility of objectives between the parties. What are the projected targets for growth? What are the new performance criteria? How autonomously will the acquired company operate? All these questions require specific answers. If the courted party is at all dissatisfied with what it is told, it should (if possible) turn the offer down.

One highly successful company I know of has been acquiring other companies for many years without attrition among the added management. This company makes it a rule that new candidates for acquisition talk to the management of previously acquired companies. This helps calm possible paranoia about what might happen after the takeover. In addition, top management of the purchasing company systematically rehearses beforehand with management of the acquired company what it will require from the new management once it is in the fold. Such an approach minimizes surprises and benefits everyone in the end.

I cannot emphasize too strongly that making mergers, acquisitions, and strategic alliances work requires a regard for the human side of things. Many of the points I made in the preceding chapter about the processes of downsizing and change hold true for mergers as well. Mergers and acquisitions arouse fundamental concerns about trust and identity and induce an enormous amount of anxiety about dealing with change. Many employees experience an overwhelming sense of confusion, disruption, and loss of control. Others suffer worries about job loss or job changes, changes in power, prestige, and status, or changes in compensation and perks.

In the face of such concerns, some of the best executives may decide to leave. Ideally, the acquiring company will have a plan outlining for its employees the specific consequences of the deal. Detailed plans go a long way toward reducing employees' anxiety. Unfortunately, my research shows that such plans are very rarely carried out.

When employees are forced to submit to far-reaching changes in the corporate environment, they must be given the opportunity to mourn the old attachments and habits that will be broken by the new alliance. Employees must come to accept the fact that things are going to be different, that the old company and their specific role in it no longer exist. In the postmerger phase, this mourning process has to be managed in a psychologically effective and humane way to avoid depressive reactions and other symptomatology.

One company I know of organized a kind of wake to mourn the loss of its original name, which was going to be changed after the merger. For many executives there, the change of name was not simply the change of a few letters but a symbol of a much deeper loss: the disappearance of the original company with which their lives had been intimately connected. Psychologically, the change could almost have been seen as an assault on the self, given the importance of the company name to the personal identity of many people who had spent the better part of their adult life with the company. A special workshop was organized where employees' newly experienced sense of discontinuity could be publicly discussed. This opportunity was very much appreciated by all concerned. Another great help to these employees in handling this emotional agenda was their participation not only in choosing a new name but also in discussing the future direction of the company. The attention given by top management to these issues contributed greatly to a smooth transition process.

To prevent anxiety from becoming explosive, it is essential that senior management keep communication channels open. Lack of clarity about expectations can lead to a cycle of escalating conflict, distrust, and polarization. At certain points in the negotiations, secrecy may have a place; but it should be dismantled as soon as possible—before it can lead to excessively political behavior. In one company (as an example of the trouble secrecy can cause), because of a false belief that sharing imperfect knowledge would only confuse middle management, top executives hoarded all the relevant information. They failed to realize that noncommunication is a negative factor of communication itself. The results were predictable. Many of the more mobile executives contacted headhunting firms. Some left, which was a great loss to the company. The situation could easily have been avoided if the transition had been managed more sensitively.

During this transitional period, it is important for the people of the acquiring company not to strut around like victorious conquerors. It is essential to preserve the dignity of the people in the acquired company and to show understanding for the strain they are under. At times it may even be advisable to appoint a kind of traffic controller to prevent a possible invasion by people from the head office. All too often when a new company is acquired, many executives from the head office deem it necessary to visit and give advice, creating even more confusion in the process.

Frequent reviews should be conducted during the transition process. They provide opportunities to discuss the reasons for the merger and to open up a dialogue about possible changes in company name, structure, and management. Natural items on the agenda include the likelihood of redundancy, reassignment of jobs, and changes in the reward structure. At these reviews, management should continue to attend to the psychological dimensions of the process of change as well.

In the initial phase of a merger or acquisition, it is also advisable to delay wielding the budget ax as long as possible. If people have to be dismissed, remember some of the earlier rules about downsizing: it should be done with dignity and generosity. People have long memories for callous behavior, and the head office has to obtain and nurture the cooperation of the people who remain.

During this period, it is essential to create cross-company task forces and project teams. The new rules of the game have to be articulated. This kind of teaming up will facilitate the problem-solving process and set the stage for future collaboration.

A good example of a very successful merger is that of ABB. After Percy Barnevik announced the merger between the Swedish company ASEA and the Swiss company Brown Boveri, he selected five key executives from each company to form a ten-member top management committee. This committee was then broken up into task forces whose brief was to analyze how the two operations could best be merged. Subsequently, 500 senior executives from both companies were interviewed to identify future key players. The criteria for selection were clearly defined at the time. The top jobs were going to risk takers, team players, and motivators. A major program was initiated to communicate the company's priorities. Barnevik personally explained his vision of the new company to ABB's 300 top executives. These people were asked to communicate his message down the line. In a very short time, the message reached 30,000 executives worldwide. As the results eventually indicated, the way the process was handled at ABB went a long way toward alleviating a high level of anxiety and contributed to the company's future success.

It is important, then, that senior executives be aware of the psychological dimensions of the merger and acquisition process and avoid distancing themselves. Indeed, they should demonstrate personal involvement. Following the example of Barnevik, they should clarify the rules of the game, especially as those rules touch on issues such as the reward structure and objectives for growth and performance. Integration should be a top priority. Again, as Barnevik did at ABB, top executives should include the relevant managers in decision-making processes. At the same time, close attention should be paid to morale and intercompany team building, and regular culture or climate audits should be held to flag possible areas of conflict.

Unfortunately, the people responsible for mergers frequently fail to pay sufficient attention to these more qualitative factors.

Employees are still subjected to mushroom treatment; more often than not, they are kept in the dark. To those who are still tempted to merge, I offer a word of caution: beware the infectiousness of merger fever; it can lead to untimely death if not treated properly.

5

Do You Like Singing
the Company Song?
Corporate Culture

*What is culture? To know what concerns one, and to
know what it concerns one to know.*

Hugo von Hofmannsthal

*Inevitably, the culture within which we live shapes
and limits our imaginations, and by permitting us
to do and think and feel in certain ways makes it
increasingly unlikely or impossible that we should
do or think or feel in ways that are contradictory
or tangential to it.*

Margaret Mead

*When I hear anyone talk of culture I reach for my
revolver.*

Hermann Göring

Before any merger or joint venture, it is well worth carrying out an audit of the respective company cultures. This means an assessment of qualitative factors such as the values, perceptions, and artifacts that regulate life in an individual organization. Prospective partners should spend time thinking about what kind of "marriage" they would like to have. Is there both a strategic *and* an organizational fit? What kind of end result do they foresee? Is it going to be a merger of equals? Are they looking for cultural pluralism, implying that the acquired company will have maximum flexibility to operate autonomously? Or is there perhaps an active wish for some form of cultural blending, with all the unpredictability that will come with it? Alternatively, is it going to be a cultural takeover, whereby the culture of the acquired firm will be replaced with that of the purchasing firm? It is vital that sufficient attention be paid to these possible scenarios.

You may have heard of school songs, but have you ever heard of company songs? Such songs are part and parcel of corporate culture. Perhaps you are raising your eyebrows in disbelief or murmuring, "Maybe in Japan." But quite a few Western companies have a company song; IBM, in fact, has a whole booklet of them! The late chairman of IBM, Thomas Watson, Sr., may well have believed that "people who sing together, stay together." And he would have had a point, given the incredible success IBM had for so many years. Surely it must do *something* to you if you sing words such as these (to the tune "Singing in the Rain") as a group:

> Selling IBM, we're selling IBM,
> What a glorious feeling, the world is our friend.
> We're Watson's great crew, we're loyal and true;
> We're proud of our job and we never feel blue.
> We sell our whole line, we're there every time,
> To chase away gloom with our products so fine.
> We're always in trim, we work with a vim,
> We're selling, just selling, IBM.

Of course, considering the company's most recent troubles, it is quite possible that IBM employees were so busy singing to themselves that they failed to notice the environment changing around them.

Corporate culture is a concept that was rarely talked about fifteen years ago. But times have changed, and now it is very rare to have a conversation with an executive and *not* hear some reference to it. How can this shifting concern be explained? What is the reason for the sudden popularity of corporate culture? After all, every individual organization, by definition of its uniqueness, has a corporate culture.

You do not have to go far to find an explanation. You need only open the financial pages of any newspaper and read the corporate war stories you find there. You are quite likely to find something about Japan straightaway. The reason for this is that perhaps the first inducement for the sudden interest shown in the concept of corporate culture was the emergence of Japanese corporations as a competitive threat. People started to ask themselves what was so different about Japanese companies, and what made them so successful.

As Japan began to attract more and more attention, management scholars Tony Athos and Richard Pascale attempted to shed some light on the phenomenon in their book *The Art of Japanese Management,* in which they presented the "seven S" diamond framework used extensively by the consulting firm McKinsey to help explain the management processes that drive a company. The McKinsey diamond is formed from seven S's: structure, staff, systems, style, skills, strategy—and in the middle, something called shared values or superordinate goals (in other words, corporate culture). For Athos and Pascale, the emphasis Japanese companies put on manipulating these shared values became the explanatory variable in clarifying the difference in effectiveness between Western and Japanese companies.

As I wrote in Chapter Four, it is also difficult to find a day without a story in the financial pages referring to mergers, acquisitions, and/or strategic alliances. Analyses of what went wrong in such situations have become quite common. Executives have begun to realize that in order to make these special relationships work, they have to go beyond simple financial calculations and look at the human factors—and corporate culture is one of those. For example, if Ciba-Geigy, a company making lifesaving drugs and fertilizers, bought a company called Carpet Fresh, there is little chance that the acquired company would fit into the corporate mold.

The need to know more about the ins and outs of corporate culture has been fueled largely by the changes in the regulatory environment and the effects of privatization. What elements of the corporate culture do you have to manipulate to change AT&T from a service-oriented telephone company to a market-oriented communications business? What does privatizing a company such as Renault really involve?

Top executives have rapidly had to realize that it is corporate culture that is the real bond between the people in an organization. Certainly, that culture transcends the directly visible aspects of organizational policy. In many companies, corporate culture has begun to be used as a subtle control device, underlying the more formal selection, planning, and control systems. It becomes the glue that holds the company together.

In the modern global corporation, it is increasingly difficult to control worldwide operations through formal systems only. There are too many ways in which those systems can be sidestepped. For example, when you send one of your executives to Papua New Guinea, can you really control what he or she is doing? Do you really know what is happening out there? Although few would admit it openly, it is impossible to know what is really going on. As a result, the control function becomes de facto more ritualistic. In many instances, people at the head office merely go through the motions; they have only an illusion of control. Here is where "softer" systems, such as corporate culture, become important. Ideally, by the time executives are sent to faraway places, they have internalized the dos and don'ts of their particular company and know very clearly what is expected of them. They know the taboos and can correctly predict what will mean instant excommunication.

When we look closer, we discover that corporate culture is a very elusive concept. Not surprisingly, then, there is considerable confusion about what people really mean when they talk about it. You cannot feel it, you cannot touch it, you cannot smell it, but you know it is there. A very basic definition is "the way we do things around here." But that is too simplistic. Perhaps it is more accurate to talk about the values and beliefs shared by the people who work in an organization. From this angle, it becomes clear that knowing the culture of a company is useful in explaining why the people in the company act in a certain way, why they believe certain things, and why they value certain things over others.

I have my own definition of organizational culture: I view it as a mosaic of basic assumptions about the world, expressed as beliefs, values, and characteristic patterns of behavior that are shared within the organization and are adopted by the organization's members in an effort to cope with both internal and external pressures.

Knowing a company's culture can be useful for a variety of reasons. It can help you understand how the strategy-making process works and give you insight about how you should handle external stakeholders. In addition, it can give you a good idea of what kind of people will fit in, the preferred style of interpersonal relations and forms of leadership in your company, and the kind of people who will do well there. Furthermore, it may give you some insight about the criteria for successful performance and advancement.

Obviously, companies with a company song are likely to have a strong culture. I have already indicated that this is not necessarily a good thing to have, however. Whether it is good or bad rather depends on the circumstances. If the company is operating in a very stable environment, a strong culture may be a good thing. However, as the case of IBM has shown, too strong a corporate culture may turn out to be a handicap in a very turbulent environment. Remember the boiled frog phenomenon? Through lack of diversity, the company may have become myopic and less good at reading the danger signs in the environment.

Of course, it is possible to escape the conundrum of strong versus weak corporate culture and have it both ways, by creating a strong corporate culture with openness to new approaches as one of its specific characteristics.

Every corporate culture begins with a person and an idea. Even in very mature organizations, if we dig deep enough, we can perceive the shadow of the founder. In many companies—for example,

Honda, IBM, ICI, Philips, Shell, and Ford—we see how the founder's philosophy lingers on long after his or her death. Over time, the philosophy of the founder is expressed through values, beliefs, and norms that become institutionalized through the kind of selection and socialization processes used by senior management.

It is not an easy task to decode the essentials of a company's culture. There is really no such thing as a quick analysis; a simple questionnaire is not going to give you all the answers. With organizational culture, you have to look for commonalities; you have to look for themes about which there is common agreement. You have to be something of an anthropologist to find out what a company's culture is all about—and an anthropologist interested in amateur detection, at that. You have to look beyond the obvious. It is not usually enough to ask the people who work in a company for the specifics of their culture. All too often, the organization's participants are quite unaware of its general ambience and unique features. They are like fish in water: fish realize the importance of water only when they are taken out of it.

The first task of the culture decoder is to look for symbols, shared codes of meaning. These symbols come in many forms. For example, what can be said about the company's architecture? What statement does it make about the company? What image does it try to present to the world? What do the buildings look like?

In one company I know, everything—even the meeting rooms—is made of glass. There is nowhere to hide. There are no places to build nests. The only places where you can find some privacy are the bathrooms and the parking lot. The glass structure and the open office design are clear statements from top management that this organization has a performance culture. Everyone is on stage. People who have applied for work in this company and then seen the architecture have been known to walk straight out, realizing that this kind of setup would not fit their personality. Not only would they prefer a certain amount of privacy; they would also like a more easygoing ambience.

Not only the design of a building but also the furnishings, the layout of the offices, and the way space is allocated say a lot about a company. Is it an open design, or do people have their own closed offices? Are there separate dining rooms and specific parking spaces for the executives? Are there separate washrooms? Does the president have his own bathroom? What other sorts of privileges are there? I have heard that PepsiCo has the ultimate symbol for the CEO: the executive fountain, an impressive construction on the lawn. The CEO can turn it on and off with a button located in his office. What is the significance of *this* sort of symbolism?

From architecture, let us turn to language. Is there a particular kind of language used in the company? Are there special terms that only insiders understand? Every organization has current expressions unique to the place, but do they predominate? Dress code is another form of language, of course. Does everyone walk around in a dark suit and a white shirt, or can people wear old sweaters (as the people in a company such as The Virgin Group can)?

And what about security? What can this tell you about a company's culture? Is it easy to enter the company, or are there elaborate security checks? In one company I know, you are practically held by the hand wherever you go. There is even someone waiting for you outside the bathroom! Heaven forbid, you may accidentally glance at a confidential file! In another company, a bank, it is even worse. The paranoid elements of that particular corporate culture are very well symbolized by the incredible difficulties visitors experience in getting in and getting out.

In addition to these major signs of corporate culture, there are plenty of small clues, such as the bulletin board, that can give important insights about the corporate culture. What kind of things can you learn from the messages left there?

Each company, of course, has its own myths, its sagas about the uniqueness of its culture. It has stories about its heroes, mythologizing certain individuals. A myth is not simply make-believe, however; it is a selection and shaping of evidence to act as a shining example, a justification of certain attitudes and policies. What myths are recounted about how people behaved when the company was in trouble? Who were the heroes who saved the day? How did they go about solving the crisis? What stories are told about the president? How do these stories influence the behavior of the people in the company?

In one very successful company I know, people are encouraged to take risks. They are given large amounts of money to set up businesses in faraway places. It is acceptable to make mistakes in this culture. There is, however, one major taboo. If you make a mistake, you have to be frank about it, bring it out into the open. The most deadly sin in this company is to try to shove a mistake under the carpet. The president of the company takes pride in the fact that he is the "donkey"; he makes it very clear that he takes the responsibility for all errors made by the company. To emphasize this point, there is a photograph hanging close to the boardroom of the president dressed like a farmer and sitting facing backward on a donkey!

Finally, there are ritualized types of behavior that can be found in any company, dramatized expressions enacted by the organizational participants. For example, how do people act at meetings? What kind of entry and exit ceremonies exist in the organization? What sort of events are celebrated? Are special events organized for people who have shown exceptional performance? A very good example of this kind of event is what happens at the cosmetics firm Mary Kay, where once a year at a big event in Dallas the most successful salespeople are crowned and given pink Cadillacs, jewelry, and fur coats as rewards.

By studying the various aspects of organizational functioning, we can identify a number of key factors that characterize the culture of a specific company. In that identification, we ask ourselves questions such as these: What degree of autonomy is allowed in the organization. To what extent is there a sense of togetherness? Do people have to operate under a lot of pressure? Do the organization's members support each other, or does the law of the jungle prevail?

Do people recognize each other's contributions? To what extent is innovation encouraged in the organization? Is creativity an important value? And one of the most important questions of all: What level of trust prevails in the organization?

We can see how, in the decoding process, we have to be like detectives going from surface to deep structure, peeling away layer after layer of the onion that is the company culture, finding in the center the core values of the original founder of the organization.

Having diagnosed the company culture, is it possible to change it? The answer is yes, it is; but as with the process of changing individuals, do not expect too much, too quickly. Despite wishes to the contrary, corporate cultures cannot be changed overnight. And lobotomies can be dangerous. Do not destroy all that has been created. It is much better to build on the strong points of an existing culture. Wiping out the corporation's history is, in most instances, not the wisest strategy.

So how can we go about effecting a culture change? One way (paradoxical as it may sound) is to do nothing. As most of us know, not doing something is also a form of action. However, this rather passive approach to the organizational environment, relying on a process of natural evolution, can be risky. Remember, if nothing has changed for a couple of years, it is time to check your company's pulse—the patient may be dead. If too many people in the company take this passive approach, the company may find itself one day suddenly irrelevant. As Freud wrote in *The Future of an Illusion*, "A culture which leaves unsatisfied and drives to rebelliousness so large a number of its members neither has a prospect of continued existence nor deserves it."

To avoid such an outcome, a much better approach is to take a more proactive stand and engage in a continual process of planned change. Obviously, it helps if people in the company experience a *need* to change, if they feel that the time has come to do things differently. And it helps even more if top management feels this need. Without the support of the power structure, one can go only so far.

Organizational development events, during which key elements of the managerial processes are examined by a company's executives, are one way of engaging in preventive maintenance. They offer a very effective way of changing the mindset of the people in a company. If a seminar is set up well, it can create strong employee commitment. I have worked actively with senior executives in many of these organizational change seminars. I usually design these events around some of the major "headaches" that preoccupy the executives. I may start by establishing some benchmarks: discussing excellent business practices at other companies that are worth imitating. The idea of benchmarks has been used to good effect by companies such as Du Pont, Milliken, Motorola, AT&T, and Xerox. It is very helpful in getting a lively discussion started. I also introduce some conceptual material about various management issues, when appropriate.

To stimulate discussion at these change seminars, I ask many questions. Among them are these: What things do people at other companies say about your organization? What things are keeping you from doing the kind of job you would like to do? What would you change first if you had the power to do so? What would *you* like to accomplish during the coming fiscal year? What does your dream organization look like? Sometimes, to loosen participants up, I ask some offbeat questions: If you were to imagine that your organization is an animal, what animal would you name? Would it perhaps be a turtle or a rhinoceros? What animal would you *like* the organization to be? Would you choose a cheetah, a racehorse, a dolphin? If your organization were a person, what would the person look like? Would it be a man or a woman, old or young, shabby or elegantly dressed? If you try asking questions such as these, you will be surprised at how quickly (and how much, behind all the nervous laughter) you learn about the organization's culture, its good and its bad sides, and what people would like to change. Obviously, these more metaphorical questions set subconscious or even unconscious processes into motion, to very good effect.

The ability to bring about even very small changes will have an empowering effect on participants in this sort of development exercise. Consequently, it is useful to build this possibility into the design of the seminar. Discussion of smaller issues can then become the basis for engaging in a more dramatic change effort. In order to facilitate this process, I usually involve top management in the last part of the organizational development effort and initiate a dialogue in which new ideas that have evolved during the seminar can be tested. This dialogue often shows whether current management practices and organizational culture still make sense in changing circumstances. Moreover, since the actual powerholders take part in the discussion, real action can be decided upon immediately.

A systems approach is another way of introducing changes in the corporate culture. As I mentioned earlier, information technology is changing the way people relate to each other. It also very much affects patterns of power and influence in the organization. Most companies have been touched one way or another by information technology. As a result, certain functions and practices have been totally dropped. For example, a thing as simple as electronic mail has radically transformed the information flow in many companies. In their turn, changes in information flow encourage much more participative work environments.

Scandal can also be a tool for change, though perhaps not by choice. When a company finds its name in the papers because of some socially unacceptable action, change in certain behavior patterns often comes about very quickly. Think of companies that have been caught polluting the environment or have been involved in bribery. For example, a major chemical spill, such as the one that occurred at the Swiss pharmaceutical firm Sandoz, can have a lasting effect on how the company conducts itself. Top executives may like to see their name in the newspaper, but not for this sort of reason.

Finally, reorganizations, mergers, and bankruptcies have to be included among the factors influencing culture change. These events involve massive replacements of people; and with these replacements, other sets of values are brought into the company. Companies such as People Express, MCA, Wang, and Barings Bank PLC have all been altered by these processes.

Knowing what you now know about corporate culture, do you want to find yourself learning the words of the company song? Or will you look for other sorts of glue to provide a sense of community and common purpose within your organization? Whatever you do, be wary of transforming a culture thoughtlessly. Do not interfere with it unless you understand what lies behind some of its features. Find out why things are done in certain ways in the organization. A company culture stands for something—and if you do not stand for something, you will fall for anything!

6

A Cultural Tower of Babel

Managing Across Borders

In Italy for thirty years under the Borgias they had
warfare, terror, murder, bloodshed—they produced
Michelangelo, Leonardo da Vinci and the Renais-
sance. In Switzerland they had brotherly love, five
hundred years of democracy and peace and what did
that produce . . . ? The cuckoo clock.

Orson Welles

As an effective leader, you may think you have figured out and even transformed your own company's corporate culture. But are you sure you have not left out an important factor: national culture? Are you perhaps being too parochial? Are you presuming that your man in Brazil is going to behave in the same way as his colleague in Germany? How will a Dutch executive react if you give her an earful about decline in sales, and how will her reaction differ from that of a British executive? How does strategic decision making differ between the Danes and the French? To what extent does national culture influence corporate culture, and vice versa?

These are important questions. If we do not give them the attention they deserve, conflict is inevitable. Recognizing differences in national culture is of vital importance in cross-border mergers, acquisitions, and joint ventures and can affect decision making, the understanding of prevailing patterns of leadership and authority, differences in motivation and control, and management of cross-cultural teams. National culture is really the filter through which we see and interpret the world around us. It influences our ways of perceiving, thinking, feeling, and evaluating. As such, it has an impact on how we are influenced by corporate culture. There is enormous cultural diversity from country to country in attitudes toward work, for example. How do executives from various national cultures regard such factors as power, authority, formalization, and hierarchy? How do their responses differ?

A colleague of mine at INSEAD, André Laurent, has done a great deal of work on these issues, and the attitude surveys he has carried out reveal great variation among these organizational variables. The question that immediately springs to mind is *why* these differences occur; but given the likely multicausality, it is not easy to answer that question. I hypothesize, however, that many of these differences originate in variations in basic perceptions about the different degrees of control people think they have over their natural environment. Basically, it is likely that a person who feels helpless vis-à-vis external forces in the environment will have a very different perception of power, authority, hierarchy, and ways of decision making than someone who possesses a strong sense of control.

These fundamental perceptions about control derive very much from variations in childrearing in different cultures. Children who are not given much discretionary space, whose parents insist that they do as they are told and not ask why, develop in a cultural situation very different from one in which explanations are given for required patterns of behavior. If developing children feel consistently helpless because they are deprived of control over their actions, this sense of impotence will persist throughout life and color their behavior as adults. Childrearing patterns will also determine the degree of trust with which people approach the environment when they are adults—another factor that has an effect on the way they deal with the business world.

To take some examples: organizational politics mean very different things for Scandinavians and people from Latin countries. For the former, organizational politics are of limited importance; Latin Europeans and Latin Americans, on the other hand, expend a considerable amount of their time and energy on political maneuvering and the pursuit of power. To the latter, organizations are political entities, and each person's organizational purpose is to maintain one's power base and control. Organizations are not considered in a more instrumental way, as bodies designed to get tasks accomplished. In Latin countries, therefore, much more attention is devoted to personal relationships than to tasks and functions. Achieving objectives often seems to be a secondary consideration. As many newcomers to the Latin European or Latin American scene have discovered the hard way, one ignores these attitudinal differences at one's own peril.

There are also great differences in the way executives from various national cultures look at issues of authority. For the French and Italians, for example, it is very important to know who has authority over whom. Authority is seen as person-related; it is an attribute of the individual. Thus functional and personal authority cannot really be differentiated. In other cultures, such as the United States or Switzerland, authority tends to be more position-related; it is an attribute of the task. In such instances, authority derives from role or function. Working across cultures, the choice between tailoring the person to the job or the job to the person becomes quite crucial.

The same problems occur when we consider hierarchy and formal processes in the organization. Job descriptions are important in some countries but carry much less weight in others. Well-defined roles and responsibilities preoccupy people in Sweden to a much lesser extent than people in countries such as France, Switzerland, or Germany. In certain countries, including the People's Republic of China, it is a major faux pas to bypass the hierarchical line. In other countries, executives cannot understand why it is such a big deal.

Imagine the effect of trying to introduce structures where sub-ordinates have two bosses in countries such as France, Italy, Indonesia, or the People's Republic of China. Such efforts at organizational design would not improve one's standing in the organization in those cultures. So much for the idea of introducing matrix structures! Given the ways in which attitudes toward work differ from culture to culture, in the global corporation this organizational type can very quickly lead to serious constipation. If you are determined to make matrix structures work, you had better engage in a dramatic cultural sensitization program designed to help people cope with the ambiguity such structures imply. But do not expect it to be easy.

So how does the process of decision making work within the different national cultures your organization encounters? Is it consensus-driven, as tends to be the case in Japan? Or is it more centralized, with decisions coming down from one individual, as we see more in Latin countries? In the former, decisions tend to be made on a step-by-step basis, less impulsively than is often the case in the latter. Moreover, in the latter we can expect to find a more autocratic leadership style.

Of course, major strategic implications can be drawn from these differences in decision making. Obviously, it takes quite some time to arrive at a decision in a Japanese company, while in many Western countries decision making can be very rapid. The catch, however, is in the implementation process: while implementation is very fast in Japanese companies (where consensus has already been reached), it takes some time in Western companies (where no consensus yet exists).

A related question is whether the ultimate aim of the organization is the good of the group, or whether the company's philosophy is that what is good for the individual will de facto be good for the group. This distinction boils down to whether people in a particular country have an individualistic orientation, meaning that they are expected to take care of themselves, or whether it is the group that occupies center stage. Countries such as the United States and Australia tend to be very individual-oriented, whereas countries such as Indonesia, Singapore, and Japan are more group-oriented. However, while the Japanese work to establish a personal relationship with the decision makers, to get to know them, this way of operating is much less important in the United States, where people try to keep the process impersonal, to *avoid* personal involvement.

In decoding cross-cultural issues, we should keep in mind that there is constant confusion between what we say, what we do, and what we mean. I have always been fond of the expression "Look at their feet," which I take to mean, "Don't take things merely at face value; consider other indicators."

I find it helpful to imagine a "culture pyramid." At the pinnacle, we find visible behavior, practices that can be observed by anybody. At the next level down, a less visible one, we find the various norms that determine the underlying systems, structures, rituals, and myths that characterize a specific national culture. Finally, buried at the base of the pyramid are the basic values and belief systems that form the foundation of the specific national culture; these are unconscious, taken for granted.

Since we are all human, we all have certain things in common. At the same time, each of us has some unique characteristics. It follows, then, that people from different cultures will have commonalities but also variances. And given similarities in upbringing, it is likely that people from similar cultures have a greater overlap in specific characteristics than people from very different cultures. Thus, while the Germans and the French may have behavioral similarities, there is likely to be a shift in emphasis from one nationality to the other concerning specific ways of looking at things. The "average" German will have certain amount of overlap with the "average" French person, but the normal distribution of individual characteristics will be somewhat different between the two nationalities.

Cultural stereotyping, or ascribing certain ways of behaving and acting to individuals of a specific culture, is based on these commonalities. Thus we have our stereotypical image of what the Italians, the

French, the Germans, and the English are like: "The Italians are the world's best lovers; they must have invented the word *romantic*." "I didn't know he was dead; I thought he was British." These stereotypes vary depending on which culture is doing the stereotyping, of course. For example, the French see Americans as industrious and energetic, while the Japanese see them as nationalistic; the British, meanwhile, view them as friendly and self-indulgent, and the Brazilians see them as intelligent, inventive, and greedy. These differences in perception make for a confusing spectrum.

In trying to understand how national culture influences corporate culture, I often find it useful to look at several kinds of "language" spoken by each group. This is a perspective used by some anthropologists and psychoanalysts. Let me explain what I mean. To begin with, I look at what I call the "language of language," the actual way people speak. Is the speech pattern a constant stream of words, or is speech punctuated by many silences? For example, compare the differences in speech between a Mexican and a Finn. Some Finns, listening to the Mexican speech pattern, are quite bewildered; they think speakers are suffering from verbal diarrhea. On their part, the Mexicans think that the Finns are verbally constipated and are likely, because of their impatience with the flow of words, to complete the Finns' sentences for them. Depending on the culture, silence can be interpreted as a sign of respect, a way to give the other party space (as in Finland), or an indication of impoliteness (as in the United States).

There is also the language of food. Every country has idiosyncratic rituals built up around eating and drinking. How should one eat? Who should be served first? Who should get the choice bits? What do certain meals stand for? How does one go about making a toast? What may seem a very simple process is bound by many rules and regulations in a country such as Sweden. What does it mean to be invited to someone's house for dinner? The significance of being invited to a U.S. home is quite different from that of being asked to eat at the house of a Japanese family.

What about the language of locomotion? What do certain postures, movements, hand gestures, facial expressions, and forms of eye contact mean in different cultures? Each culture has its own way of sitting, standing, reclining, and gesturing. For example, the uninformed observer will interpret the way an Indian shakes his head as a no, while it actually means a yes. And what does it mean when a French person blows out air in an exaggerated manner?

Then there is the language of emotion. How are emotions dealt with in different cultures? The Japanese, for example, tend to hide emotions (at least it seems so to Western eyes), and they are not inclined to touch each other publicly. In contrast, people from Latin America tend to be emotionally demonstrative; touching and embracing are intrinsic parts of their culture. In general, men in the United States and Western Europe avoid excessive touching (although women are more demonstrative); they keep their distance and are more controlled. This in turn is quite different from the behavior of people from Arab countries, who tend to be more demonstrative.

What about the language of time? Some anthropologists like to make a distinction between "doing" and "being" cultures. In the former, the perception of time is that it is limited: time is money. Consequently, people in these cultures have a task-oriented approach. To be on time and keep to schedules are overriding concerns. In contrast, for people from "being" cultures, time is unlimited, plentiful. It is regarded as space for relating; hence the attitude toward time is much more flexible. Not surprisingly, people from such cultures tend to be late. Imagine a Swede being invited to dinner by an Italian. The script runs as follows: Ten minutes before the agreed-upon time, we can expect to see the Swede (who comes from a "doing" culture) walking nervously around the block, looking at his watch. Exactly on the dot he will ring the bell, to find that his hostess is still in the bathtub. Given her cultural expectations, she presumed he would arrive at least an hour later.

Of course, the management of time also indicates how important you are. In Arab countries, important people get quicker service than less important ones. Time spent waiting in the office of an executive in many countries may be a not-so-subtle reminder of how important the person who keeps you waiting thinks he or she is.

We also have the language of space. In the United States, proximity authorizes familiarity, which makes for easygoing, neighborly relationships. But try the same behavior patterns in a country such as France. There people do not just drop in! This distinction is also reflected in organizational attitudes. The French are much less inclined than Americans to knock unannounced on another person's office door, even if it is nearby.

In the United States, the more important an executive is, the bigger the office (and preferably in a corner on the top floor). For the Japanese, the action tends to be centered around the middle of the building. For the people of India, the sense of space is very different from that of people in the West. What may seem a cramped office to a Western eye may look very spacious to an Indian. The same can be said about distance in the context of commuting. What may seem like a major expedition to a Dutch worker (whose country is very small) may represent an agreeable commute to a Californian.

Linked to the issues of space and distance is the question of what is an acceptable personal distance. How physically close can you come to someone else before it becomes uncomfortable? The importance of this kind of spatial distance was brought home to me many years ago by a Spanish colleague. The two of us were standing in a hallway when he approached me to discuss a particular teaching problem. But he was too close. I felt uncomfortable about the distance; he was intruding on my private space. I backed away to get more breathing space, only to be followed by him. This scene repeated itself a number of times until I finally realized what was going on. So I stopped. Obviously, the minimum distance for the Dutch is somewhat larger than that for Spaniards. Students of this phenomenon have suggested that the regular business distance in Western countries is between one and a half and two and a half meters, while personal space ranges from fifty centimeters to a meter.

And what can be said about the language of things? What do possessions mean in different cultures? What is the relative symbolic meaning of buildings, cars, office furniture, and so on? To possess a Rolls Royce or a corporate jet is a sure sign of success in many places. But what about other perks? What does a dacha count for? Or a herd of cattle? Each culture has its own signifiers, whether subtle or unsubtle.

And we should not forget the language of friendship. Will it be easy to make friends, as it is in the United States, or will it take a long time? Does friendship mean a rather superficial relationship, or does it imply a much deeper obligation? In some countries, friends become a form of social insurance; they are people you can ask support of when times are bad. In many other cultures, that is certainly not the case.

Then there is the language of agreement. In some countries, when a deal is made, it is a deal—sealed and settled. In other cultures, it is a kind of a roadmap, the beginning of a relationship. That being the case, you can imagine the frustration and bewilderment arising from a negotiation between a Finn (for whom an agreement is chiseled in stone) and a Greek. In the United States and Western Europe, there are standard prices for most goods. In other countries, you bargain beforehand; otherwise, you leave yourself wide open to abuse and may be in for quite a surprise. (Think about something as simple as hiring taxis in such countries!)

So, after this whirlwind tour around the Tower of Babel that represents national culture, where do you find yourself? Are you even more confused? If you are, it may be a good sign. Recognizing your own ignorance tends to be excellent preventive medicine against cultural arrogance.

Are You Sure You Want to Work Abroad?

International Assignments

Few people can be happy unless they hate some other person, nation, or creed.

Bertrand Russell

You have just agreed to run the company's entire Far Eastern operation. This kind of proposition was far from your mind when you were asked to attend the last board meeting. Top management must have recognized the quality of your work. What a great career opportunity!

But wait a moment. Did you get the whole picture? They talked about the advantages at the board meeting, but what about the drawbacks? You have some experience with cross-cultural organizational issues, but how is this move going to affect you personally? Are you sure you asked the right questions? Did you really cover all the aspects of what an international assignment involves? And what will your spouse say? What about his or her own career; will there be opportunities in the host country? If not, can you afford to do without two incomes? Your spouse may well like a change of scenery, but—hold on—have you thought about your parents-in-law? Your family has always been very close to them. They are not young any longer. Will your spouse feel able to leave them? What about friends? And your children, how will they react? So many questions, and so little time!

Every day, this scenario takes place in offices around the world, and it is becoming more and more common: international assignments are now the order of the day. An international perspective is a sine qua non for an executive, given the globalization of the marketplace. It is essential for the survival of any major firm.

But we must take into consideration the human implications for the executives who have been offered such international assignments. What preparation should they be given? What are the problem areas? And what can we learn from the experiences of others who have worked abroad?

In my management programs at INSEAD, I often ask executives about the pros and cons of taking on international assignments. Although most participants recognize the importance of such assignments, in general their reactions are somewhat mixed. Over the years, I have heard quite a few horror stories about how companies have taken advantage of executives' naïveté, failing to inform them of what a particular move really involved. The company's promises and the actual situation have frequently turned out to be two very different things. Moreover, in many instances, organizations have offered no form of preparation for the foreign assignment at all. People have been sent abroad because they had a certain technical competence, period. For example, as engineers, they were known to be good at setting up new plants; others, as accountants, had successfully cleaned up a financial mess at a subsidiary. Their sensitivity to cross-cultural issues (or lack thereof)—without which all their technical know-how counted for nothing—has been ignored.

I have not received the impression, however, that the awful experiences I have heard about were deliberately contrived, malicious acts. On the contrary, at their root was generally plain ignorance. The people at the head office who were responsible for the moves had not really thought the matter through.

Other war stories I have heard have dealt with attempts to refuse a foreign assignment—often an impossibility given the culture existing in an organization. Quite a few companies are unforgiving about such refusals. Many executives have told me that such a decision would remain a black mark in their personnel file. There are differences, however. In some companies, executives can refuse once, but that's it. If they persist in refusing, it is a sure bet that they will be taken off the fast track, their career at a dead end.

Still other executives—some of those who agreed to a distant posting—have talked about culture shock and a multitude of personal factors that negatively affected their adjustment. Going to a new culture inevitably involves a disturbance of one's mental map. The safe, familiar beacons of the home country are missing. There is a whole set of different indicators, whether auditory, visual, or olfactory. This can be very disconcerting.

This initial confusion is inevitable, and the success or failure of a foreign assignment is therefore dependent on the family's—and particularly the spouse's—capacity to adapt. One important factor for success is the ability to transfer pleasurable activities from the native environment to the foreign one. For example, if family members have always enjoyed salmon fishing in Scotland, they may like fishing for dorado and peacock bass in the Amazon when posted to Brazil. Of course, less esoteric pastimes may be easier to transfer to the host culture.

In foreign assignments, satisfaction with life and family relationships is the most critical factor to effectiveness in the workplace. This factor is important in local assignments too—but less so. Many studies have demonstrated that social support is an essential buffer against stress.[1]

Unfortunately, the scenario after the move is all too often the following: First, there is a kind of honeymoon phase, with both parties—the executive and the spouse—quite excited about the experience of being in a new country. But this phase is temporary. Soon the reality of the new state of affairs hits home. One of the partners is quickly absorbed in work and frequently absent, either traveling or putting in long hours at the office. Many foreign assignments involve dealing with critical and urgent problems in a subsidiary and are extremely time-consuming; they demand a person's focus at a time when he or she is most needed at home.

The process is frequently exacerbated by the spouse's inability to find work or continue studying. The spouse ends up in limbo, left to cope alone, perhaps dealing with servants (a new experience for most Westerners) and having to build a whole new network of relationships with few opportunities to make acquaintances and build friendships.

The probable outcome, which may be called culture shock, is symptomized by the spouse's developing negative feelings about the host culture and its people. The new culture is blamed for everything that goes wrong. (Of course, culture shock tends to be more or less severe depending on the cultural complexity of the place one is sent to.) At the same time, strong feelings of nostalgia emerge about the home country and the friends and family left behind. The consequence of all this is that not infrequently the marriage relationship suffers. Alcohol or drug addiction is also not uncommon.

Students of the expatriation process estimate that between 20 and 50 percent of such assignments turn out to be failures, with failure defined as premature return. And these failures can be extremely costly, particularly since it has been estimated that the expense of maintaining an executive abroad (given all the special allowances and benefits) is two to three times higher than maintaining the person in his or her home country. For certain countries—Japan, for example—the cost is even greater.[2]

When I go back through my notes and look at the reasons given by executives for not taking on a foreign assignment, I find the most common are these: disturbance of the children's education, disruption of the spouse's career, the fear of being forgotten at the corporate center, and difficulties with repatriation. Let us look at each of these in turn.

Apart from the stress of relocating to unfamiliar surroundings and the hardships of breaking up ties of friendship, a major factor that often turns into a constraint and makes a move difficult is schooling. While children are quite mobile in nursery or primary school, the picture changes when they reach secondary school. Moves become particularly problematic when children have reached the critical years of preparing for their final exams and making a choice about what kind of higher education they want to pursue.

In certain cultures, such as that of Great Britain, where there is a tradition of sending children to boarding school, the situation may be different; children can be schooled in the home country while the parents are abroad. In many other cultures, however, parents like to have their children around as long as possible. In such instances, boarding school is a last resort.

The second factor, which has become increasingly important and is frequently a hindrance to international assignments, is the career of the spouse. The time when there was only one breadwinner in the family (usually the male) is long gone in many cultures, and the dual-career family has arrived on the scene. Despite all the positive effects of this development, certain multinational companies look at it as a disadvantage, since it affects their executives' mobility. Here, paradoxically, executives from more traditional cultures (where the wife stays at home) may be at an advantage.

Particularly among Westerners, work-oriented spouses may be reluctant to go abroad, since their own career may suffer. Even if spouses are willing to move (with the expressed wish to continue working), many countries make it very hard for them to obtain a work permit. Furthermore, if the spouse is a professional (a doctor, dentist, or lawyer), lengthy reeducation may be needed to meet the country's licensing requirements. To add insult to injury, in certain countries women are discriminated against, making a move even more unattractive for female spouses.

In any case, the time is long gone when companies could move their executives around like military personnel. Today's executives will not accept such treatment, nor will they run the risk that their spouse will not follow them abroad. Is that what the company really wants? Like it or not, the mobility of the spouse has become an important criterion in assessing a person's part in the international executive manpower pool.

The third factor, no less critical, has to do with the political implications of losing touch with the head office. In too many companies, the rule is this: out of sight, out of mind. Leaving the corporate center can be very risky indeed. Many executives have learned the hard way that being absent from the corridors of power can have a damaging effect on their career. Consequently, a non–head office assignment in some companies is equated with being sent to Siberia.

Last but not least, there are difficulties with repatriation. Repatriates frequently experience a reentry culture shock. Many companies are simply not very good at handling the process of return. All too often there is no plan for dealing with the returning executive. After a period of significant responsibility and independence—a period during which the international executive has become used to rubbing shoulders with the economic and social elite of the host country—he or she is frequently left floating, with either no specific job waiting or a job much less interesting and responsible than the one just vacated.

Numbers vary, but it has been estimated that almost 50 percent of the companies faced with the expatriate/repatriate problem have difficulty retaining their executives upon reentry.[3] Such attrition can be very costly, given the amount of money companies invest in international experience for their executives. It can also be viewed as an incredible waste of essential executive expertise. Ironically, some multinationals seem to be training their high flyers for positions in other companies.

The lack of structure and the absence of a well-thought-through career path to which to return are certainly factors that aggravate the psychological confusion to be expected when an expatriate returns. Repatriation shock experienced by executives returning to their parent organization has never received the attention it deserves. Senior management does not realize that for many repatriates, it is very hard suddenly to become a small fish in a big pond after having been a big fish in a small pond for so many years.

Losing whatever special social status an expatriate executive may have had as representative of a multinational corporation in a foreign country often contributes to repatriation shock. The discontinuation of the special benefits received while abroad may be a factor as well. It is hard to give up extras such as private schooling for the children (paid for by the company), housing subsidies, cost-of-living bonuses, a chauffeur, and domestic help.

When returning expatriates express disappointment about what has been arranged for them on their return to the home office (an arrangement that may not be at all what they had envisioned when originally sent abroad), the company frequently perceives that they are behaving like spoiled brats. Whether their disappointment is reasonable or not, the result is that repatriates feels like misfits. And so, as I have mentioned before, quite a few leave the company soon after their return.

Some expatriate executives may decide not to return at all. Having observed the experiences of some of their colleagues faced with a similar predicament, many may be aware of what they are in for if they do return. If they prefer not to go through all that upheaval themselves, and if they like their life abroad, they may decide to stay where they are and look for another job in the host country instead.

What can be done about this expatriate/repatriate problem? What steps can a company take to make expatriation more of a constructive experience for everyone?

First of all, top executives in the company should make it very clear to all concerned that taking on an international assignment is an essential part of the path to senior management. In companies such as Shell and Schlumberger, for example, every entering executive knows what he or she is in for. These employees are made quite aware at the outset that a large part of their career is going to be spent away from their respective home countries. Top management stresses the point that without international experience, an executive cannot be in the running for a senior position. It helps if top management has gone through the same experience, both as proof of its necessity and as evidence that senior executives understand what such a move implies. International assignments should be coveted and interpreted as a sign that one is in the running. This kind of career path management may be much more important than trying to bribe people with special allowances in order to entice them to go abroad. It also implies that management has to be even more careful in selecting which people are suitable for this career route.

Second, when organizations are dealing with someone who is part of a couple, both parties should be consulted. Furthermore, the company should realize that the couple may need time to prepare adequately for such a move. Both parties may need help, and in most instances company assistance is much appreciated. A typical program of assistance should cover such factors as career planning for both executive and spouse, education for the children, housing, financial matters (including taxation), and medical matters. In my experience, more and more companies that profess to be, or are trying to become, global are taking this route, and with a very positive effect. The many expatriate couples I have talked with found this kind of preparation extremely beneficial.

In addition, both parties should visit the place of work abroad and meet the people employed there in order to get a better idea of what the move is all about. Moreover, when the couple decides to go, regular home visits paid for by the company should be part and parcel of the package.

However, the bottom line is that both parties in a dual-career family should have the opportunity to think through the effect of such a move on the other's career in order to prevent later discontent. And, since the dual-career family is here to stay, companies should make more of an effort to find a suitable working arrangement for the other party. Naturally, this implies obtaining working papers. Companies must also accept that, given the working situation of the spouse, some couples are simply unable to move. When a partner in a dual-career family does not want to move, that decision should not become an indelible black mark in the executive's career file. Talking with many senior human resource people of global companies, I have seen a shift on this issue over the years. More and more of them are prepared to accept certain limiting life situations and make the appropriate accommodations.

If an executive accepts a foreign assignment, it helps if he or she goes through some kind of cultural preparation program. European and Japanese companies seem to have more experience in organizing such activities than their U.S. counterparts. Such a program should be directed at both partners and should preferably include some language training. In addition, the acquisition of a certain amount of familiarity with the customs of the country in question is a major necessity. Some of the larger global companies may have in-house facilities where they address these problems; others handle training by subcontracting arrangements with institutions that specialize in these issues.

Two kinds of mentorship—one mentor at the head office and one at the foreign desk—are also highly recommended to smooth the expatriation and repatriation process. The first type (he or she could be a member of the executive board, perhaps, or another senior executive) is assigned the task of keeping the lifeline open, informing the expatriate about developments at the head office. This person should also be charged with making the process of reentry smooth. The main task of the mentor at the foreign location is to ease the expatriation process. Such a colleague can be extremely helpful in facilitating relocation. Although ideally this mentor is a person who has firsthand knowledge of the process, having been through the same experience, he or she does not necessarily have to be another expatriate; this mentor can be a local person. For example, I know of a global Japanese financial investment company whose director of European operations (not Japanese) takes on this role, being fairly familiar with both Japanese culture and the European environment.

The mentor at the head office should take an active role in finding a proper match for the expatriate executive when he or she returns. To ensure that the organization makes use of the repatriate's enriched experience, the head office should avoid adopting a firefighting mode, one that necessitates a last-minute scramble to find an opening for the returning executive. Instead, the head office should undertake proactive career planning; human resource professionals should take an active role in monitoring the career of each organizational high flyer.

In the end, we are left with the question of whether taking on a foreign assignment is worth all the hassles involved. I think it is. A foreign assignment offers us a great opportunity to enrich our horizons. It helps us to get out of the rut many of us find ourselves in. Being out of the home environment can stimulate us to see things differently. We may discover new things about ourselves. Most important, in a time of frequent transnational mergers and joint ventures, executives increasingly find that being good at what they do in their home market is no longer enough. Only with experience in foreign assignments can an executive become a truly global leader.

8

Do You Have the Right Stuff?

The Making of a Global Leader

*The battle of Waterloo was won on the playing fields
of Eton.*

Duke of Wellington

*Look over your shoulder now and then to make sure
somebody is following.*

Henry Gilmer

There are obvious reasons why the issues of international assignments and corporate culture just discussed are becoming ever
more important to businesspeople. The world is changing. Borders
are disappearing. Traditional home-market advantages are no longer
the recipe for success. Protective trade practices have become less
acceptable, and business has become a competitive game played on
an international playing field. In this new and rapidly changing
world, another type of leader is needed—a person who has the ability to transcend national and cultural boundaries. Thus the global
leader enters the stage.

Are there any characteristics that differentiate global executives
from more common mortals? What is really special about them?
What are some factors that assist the development of a global leader?

I tried to find out what kind of new man or woman we are dealing with by taking a survey of some 300 executives involved in

international programs at INSEAD. I wish I could say that the results of this survey are earth-shattering, but unfortunately this is not so. In fact, the insights derived from my survey are rather humdrum. As a matter of fact, many characteristics that *any* effective executive should have were put forward by the respondents as necessary, in addition to some characteristics unique to global leaders. This is not so remarkable, considering the literature available on leadership. Not only are there over seventy published definitions of leadership, but there are also around 18,000 words found in the English language that are used to describe various leadership traits.

As I have said before, there is some modest agreement among researchers concerning what traits are required for effective leadership. The most commonly recognized qualities are conscientiousness, energy, intelligence, dominance, self-confidence, openness to experience, emotional stability, and task-relevant knowledge. These traits being applicable to any leader, global or local, I would like to make a few observations about what, according to my survey, is specific for the *global* leader.

First of all, and most obviously, it is important to have a solid understanding of the international socioeconomic and political scene. Those with a strong grasp of different countries' economic and cultural history are obviously more likely to succeed as global leaders than head-in-the-sand types who look no further than their own organization. Many of the top executives I have met at companies such as BP, Rhône-Poulenc Rorer, ABB, Schlumberger, Nedlloyd, Repola, and SHV very much fit this successful profile. These globetrotting top executives have a remarkable understanding of the economic and cultural history of the countries in which they are operating.

Second, global leaders need to have a healthy dose of interpersonal and transcultural sensitivity (as described earlier). Naturally, with the explosion of enterprises in the service sector, interpersonal sensitivity has become increasingly important. But given the emergence of the global corporation, interpersonal sensitivity alone is no longer good enough. A genuine affinity for other cultures (which I believe is acquired through curiosity about how people live in other parts of the world), combined with good listening and observation skills, is essential. A certain tolerance for ambiguity and a lack of dogmatism are assets as well. The executives with whom I talked at SHV (a large Dutch-based multinational in energy and distribution), for example, impressed me with their intricate knowledge of the various countries in Latin America and the Pacific Rim—major operating bases for this global operation.

What it boils down to is that the global leader must have a sense of *cultural relativity*. He or she needs to understand that there is not just one way of doing things. An ethnocentric view no longer has any place in organizational life (if it ever had). It has become increasingly clear that there is a synergistic effect in integrating and transferring practices from other cultures. If you want to be effective in leading an international team, if your marketing strategy is going to be relevant in a different cultural environment, the incorporation of other points of view becomes essential. After all, we are living in the era of the "glocal" corporation. To be successful, you have to think globally and act locally. People such as Percy Barnevik of ABB, Carlo de Benedetti of Olivetti, and Paul Fentener Van Vlissingen of SHV are good examples of this new type of leader. They have lived in other cultures, have a great sensitivity to other cultures, and know how to use the strengths of each culture to good advantage.

Another factor that stood out in my survey was the need to have a solid sense of self: individuals who succeed globally know who they are, and they know their roots (whether monocultural or multicultural). This self-confidence gives them the capacity to adapt to new situations or new cultures without losing their sense of identity. One of the risks of not having a stable identity is the impulse to "go native" when abroad. A person who reacts this way turns into a kind of chameleon, pushing his or her original heritage totally aside. Of course, another reaction is the concern (in some cases turning into panic) that another culture will disrupt one's own sense of cultural identity. An individual who experiences this reaction will do everything in his or her power to remain insulated from the unfamiliar environment. He or she may end up living in an artificial bubble, as is the case with so many Japanese executives living abroad. The most effective executives tend to be the ones who can do both: retain a sense of their own cultural roots while at the same time adopting practices from the other culture.

A final factor isolated by the survey is the desire and ability to speak other languages. It is important to remember that language is the crystallization of culture. To again cite the examples of Percy Barnevik, Carlo de Benedetti, and Paul Fentener Van Vlissingen, these global leaders can converse in many different languages.

I should mention as a caveat here that the Anglo-Saxons surveyed were not as convinced of this final point as other national groups. (After all, English is the international language.) However, if native English speakers do not make an effort in this direction, it is at their own risk. They will never be able to deal as effectively with people from different cultures as those people who try. They should not forget that the essence of a culture is reflected in its language.

The question is, How do you acquire the kind of leadership characteristics listed? Are global (or even more pedestrian local) leaders born or bred? Can just anybody become a global leader?

For the optimists who would like to hear an affirmative answer to that last question, there is the example of the Dalai Lama. Imagine this: As a child aged two, the son of modest farmers, for one reason or another correctly identifies some objects belonging to the deceased thirteenth Dalai Lama. With great acclaim, the child is consequently recognized as the spiritual leader's reincarnation. Before he knows it, together with his family he is whizzed off to Lhasa, the capital of Tibet, and formally enthroned in the Potala Palace. There he is confronted with a weighty curriculum in Buddhist studies and dialectics. And lo and behold, fifty-one years later it is obvious how this education has paid off. The person who was once a farmer's son is celebrated as a great global statesman and honored with the Nobel Peace Prize. This formula for creating a leader (global or otherwise) sounds relatively simple; however, the Dalai Lama's case is a special one because of its religious nature.

The case of the Dalai Lama is also a perfect example of the controversy of nature-nurture. It brings us back to the original question of whether leaders are born or bred. I do not have the answer, and discussions around this topic usually end in deadlock, unfortunately. The only thing I can say is that, as with most things, the truth probably lies somewhere in between. Genetic factors, such as physiological hardiness and level of energy, help. Leaders are subjected to a lot of stress in the expanding world we live in. It certainly is not helpful to have poor health. However, equally important is the development of leadership abilities at an early age. This, I believe, is dependent on the kind of care a child receives.

Since we are trying specifically to understand the development of the global leader, I want to refer to a childhood factor I have never seen mentioned in the leadership literature. This is called "stranger sociability."[1] The ease with which an infant or child deals with strangers is highly dependent on the security of the infant-mother attachment. Secure children are more likely to react positively to initial encounters with strangers. They tend to be more socially responsive to unfamiliar adults and exhibit a greater playfulness and a cooperative spirit. And here mothers in particular, as primary caretakers, play an important role—one that extends beyond the initial infant-mother attachment. Do they encourage the developing child in his or her activities? Do they give the child enough transitional space to allow for play and creativity? How do they deal with narcissism? Do these mothers help establish a solid base of self-esteem?

It can be argued, then, that the foundation is laid at an early age for the way that adults deal with unknown situations. Because of their originally secure attachment ties, some individuals will be more comfortable in dealing with people from other cultures—a definite asset for a global leader. One can thus postulate a relationship between the solidity of a person's self-esteem and the degree of culture shock experienced when going abroad.

Assume that you have the right stuff; suppose that you have what it takes. An appropriate narcissistic base has been laid, and stranger anxiety is not a problem. All the signs indicate that you have leadership potential. What other factors will help you in developing into a global leader?

A clear advantage is having had early exposure to other cultures. Leaders who were the children of parents coming from two very different cultures, for example, enjoy this advantage. It is likely that more than one language will have been spoken in their home and that the children will have visited the countries of the respective parents, encountering all the different impressions that go with them. A sense of cultural relativity will have been acquired from an early age by these people. The same can be said of the sons and daughters of diplomats and the children of expatriates brought up in a foreign culture. Many of the students at INSEAD have this kind of background, which not only helps them to survive the trials and tribulations of this very international school but (as I discovered in talking with former students many years later) seems to contribute considerably to their success in reaching leadership positions in global organizations.

A background similar to one of those mentioned above may be an advantage, but sometimes it comes at a high price. Some people experience problems centered around their sense of cultural identity: they no longer know who they really are or where they belong. In such cases, a very strong, supportive home environment becomes a great plus, serving as a buffer against this kind of confusion.

Another strategy for encouraging an interest in other cultures in one's children—an interest that may blossom into global leadership ability—is sending them on summer exchange programs. Through talking to global executives, I have discovered that their interest in other cultures in many cases began with such experiences.

Another enhancing factor in the making of the global leader is an international executive education. A place such as INSEAD, which has no real national identity, becomes an ideal breeding ground for attitudes of cultural relativity. The success of many of the graduates, who as global business leaders are able to operate in many different cultures, speaks for itself. David Simon, the chairman of BP, and Lindsay Owen-Jones, the chairman and CEO of L'Oréal, are good examples.

At INSEAD, the work takes place not only in the classrooms but also in study groups, which are very active and important. Imagine the kind of a learning experience you would have spending ten months in a group made up of one American, one French citizen, one Japanese, one Swede, one Brazilian, and one Italian. This grouping of students is a highly effective way of getting to understand other people's cultures better. A lot of knowledge about how to handle cross-cultural negotiation is picked up along the way, above and beyond the international network that is built.

What can the organization itself do to facilitate leadership among its people? Once a person with leadership potential has been hired, it is essential that he or she be given a specific assignment in another culture and be granted full responsibility for the success of that project. (I call such career assignments "doing a Timbuktu.") International assignments should be seen as an important part of one's professional development, and such career moves should have strong backing of the CEO and members of the executive committee. Of course, some of you may argue that giving a young person concrete project responsibility is too risky. Sure enough, that young person is going to make mistakes. But so what? It is the best investment you can make for the future of your company. That is the way people learn. (Remember, when people do not make mistakes, they are not making any valid decisions either.) Eventually, these early career experiences will turn out to be invaluable to leaders.

Over and over again, when I interview global business leaders and ask them where they learned how to lead, they tell stories about how, in their late twenties or early thirties, they were sent to Argentina, Taiwan, Australia, or Canada to set up a plant, restructure a sales office, arrange a joint venture—you name it. They sweated taking on the assignment, they had sleepless nights over it, and they made mistakes. But most important, they were thrilled and they learned! The lessons learned while they were on their own, having to make the project work, were never forgotten. The experience taught them an incredible amount about motivation, decision making, and taking responsibility.

Exposure to an international work environment where mentors with a global mindset can be found is another asset. After all, most successful executives have had a mentor (even if they do not always acknowledge it later in life). In global companies such as Shell, Alcatel, Unilever, ABB, and Schlumberger, you do not have to look far to find some of these ingredients of an international work environment.

However, for those people who aspire to running a global empire, it should be said that doing so can also do unhealthy things to one's sense of self-importance. Traveling by Concorde, making whirlwind visits from country to country, and having large welcoming parties waiting for you at every airport to say, "Hail to the chief!" can be an incredibly inflating experience. Hence global leaders, more than other leaders, need to remind themselves who they are and guard against becoming too puffed up. If you have reached that position, maybe you should remember what I like to call the "three H's" of leadership: a sense of humility, a sense of humanity, and above all a sense of humor. As someone who obviously had some knowledge about leadership once said to me, "Any time you think you possess power as a leader, try to order someone else's dog around!"

9

· ·

When the Future Is Now
Leadership for the Next Millennium

*To accomplish great things, one must be with the
people, not above them.*

Montesquieu

*I myself have accomplished nothing of excellence
except a remarkable and, to some of my friends,
unaccountable expertness in hitting empty ginger ale
bottles with small rocks at a distance of thirty paces.*

James Thurber

The journey, not the arrival, matters.

Michel de Montaigne

Charles Kettering once said, "My interest is in the future because I am going to spend the rest of my life there." Fortunately, the future arrives one day at a time. The last thing you want to discover is that your vision of tomorrow is already outdated. However, it is important to bear in mind that what is excellent business practice today may be dysfunctional tomorrow. Thus this collection of essays on leadership would not be complete without a look at management trends. But what *are* some of the new trends in management? What should a study of the future of excellence take into consideration?

For the last ten years or so, *excellence* has been the favorite buzz-word of the business press. Ever since 1982, when Tom Peters and

Robert Waterman's book *In Search of Excellence* was published, the fascination with the concept of excellence has persisted. Just look in the business section of any bookstore. Titles incorporating the word *excellence*, or something similar to it, are to be found everywhere.

Beneath all the hype around the concept of excellence, Peters and Waterman did have a point. They succeeded in focusing attention on the slipping competitive position of many companies participating in the global business Olympics. In many ways, their study was a ray of hope: it offered ways of dealing with the problem by looking at the characteristics that highly successful companies have in common.

Do you still remember the characteristics of excellence outlined by Peters and Waterman? For old time's sake, let us go over their ideas again. Do you remember concepts such as a bias toward action, the need to stay close to the customer, the requirements of autonomy and entrepreneurship, the principle of getting productivity through people, the need for shared values, the importance of remaining with the businesses the company knows best, the simple form and lean staff, and the simultaneous loose and tight controls? All very sensible points.

You may recall that Peters and Waterman listed a whole range of companies to prove these points. But an April 16, 1984, *Business Week* article, entitled "Who Is Excellent Now?" showed that at least fourteen of the forty-three companies on that list had already lost most of their luster of excellence. Companies such as Atari and Revlon were experiencing significant problems. Eleven years later, the situation has changed even more. Of course, this is quite understandable, since companies are not static entities; they are living systems. Believe it or not, the average life span of large industrial companies is only around forty years. A disconcerting idea, isn't it?

Motion within the league table of the business world is reflected in *Fortune*'s annual ranking of the most admired corporations. This list demonstrates the fickleness of business life, where today's success becomes tomorrow's failure. For example, IBM, having been crowned number one for years on end, fell to 8th position in 1987, dropped further to 32nd place in 1991, then slid to 281st place in 1995. IBM's dramatic fall in position (according to the people who did the ranking) was due to its inability to innovate sufficiently and recognize where the market was going. Some companies, however, such as Hewlett-Packard, Rubbermaid, and 3M, have been able to hang on in top positions year after year.

How does *Fortune* arrive at these results? The magazine polls more than 10,000 top executives, outside directors, and financial analysts and gets a good rate of response. In its search for excellence, the magazine looks at such attributes as quality of management, quality of products or services, innovativeness, long-term investment value, financial soundness, community and environmental responsibility, use of corporate assets, and the ability to attract, develop, and keep talented people.

To add spice to the poll, *Fortune* does not look only at the companies at the top but also at those at the bottom of the heap. This creates real potential for distress. How would you like to find yourself on *Fortune*'s annual shame list and be asked to explain why?

In fact, companies that survive throughout the years rather than follow the more typical cycle of start-up, growth, plateau, decline, and failure (just look at the companies on *Fortune*'s list from thirty years ago and you will discover that a large number are no longer in existence) tend to have rather conservative financial policies, possess a strong corporate culture, keep in close touch with their environment (that is, listen carefully to their customers), and have a willingness to push power down to lower levels in the organization. These companies are great believers in institutional learning, in creating an environment where some form of continuity is established between the generation presently in power and the next group of executives.

Peters and Waterman's study of excellence was merely a snapshot of current business practices. But executives should also pay attention to future trends, as I have noted. They must make an effort to find out how business will be conducted in the future and to discover the new areas in which companies will need to excel.

As the year 2000 looms ahead, certain future developments seem to be inevitable. For example, executives will have to pay an increasing amount of attention to the social, economic, political, and physical environment. A company ignores the warning signs from these areas at its own peril; the time of living in splendid isolation is long past. Public environmental awareness has grown rapidly, and this has to be reflected in company policy. The *Exxon Valdez* and Bhopal disasters have taught companies a valuable lesson. Many pharmaceutical and chemical companies now have institutionalized crisis management teams to deal with ecological catastrophes. Other industries are reacting similarly. Car companies are scrambling to develop cleaner engines. Power-generation industries are becoming increasingly effective in using antipollution devices. Waste-recycling companies are hot items on the stock market. The list goes on. The need for greater environmental sensitivity means that companies will have to experiment with different forms of accounting that take these ecological issues into consideration.

The rise of the global or transnational corporation, the merger and acquisition phenomenon, and the explosion of international strategic partnerships (combined with an increase in service industries) impose a great need for training in interpersonal and cross-cultural management skills. Obviously, to make these new organizational combinations work, "softer" qualities—skills in such areas as cultural empathy, listening, communication, and motivation—must be mastered. These skills will be essential for companies that aspire to excellence. The world is becoming smaller, and cultural blends are now the rule rather than the exception. An ethnocentric orientation is entirely inappropriate. The claim that one country's way of doing things is the only right way is an invitation to disaster.

The growing mobility of personnel means dealing with an ever-greater diversity of ethnic origin and value systems in the workforce and a growing contribution from women. There is no place for sexism in management. Obviously (and I will say more about this in Chapter Ten), the increasing number of women in senior positions will significantly affect our way of running organizations in the future.

Some men, however, for a number of psychological reasons, still find it difficult to deal with women in a position of superiority. Having women as secretaries is one thing; having them as bosses is another story altogether. Companies whose executives are susceptible to these psychological problems may be at a competitive disadvantage.

There is another psychologically based trend that should be considered: some cultural historians claim that we are currently living in an age of narcissism, and psychiatrists report that the incidence of narcissistic disorders is increasing. Rapid social change and the accompanying breakdown of traditional social structures may explain this occurrence. As the compensating function of social structure disappears, these disorders seem to be on the rise. Excessive self-centeredness and self-reference are among the characteristics of narcissistically based disturbances. The people who are now entering corporations are part of what the novelist Thomas Wolfe has described as the "'me' generation." They do not ask what they can do for the organization; instead, they ask what the organization can do for them. The concept of corporate loyalty has been thrown out of the window.

This preoccupation with the self implies a greater concern with self-renewal and career change. The organization man who strongly identified with his company—the model for many years—is rapidly becoming an anachronism. Lifetime employment in one company is increasingly rare. Two factors that have accelerated this process are the phenomena of corporate downsizing and business process reengineering. These developments do not encourage corporate loyalty. As a result of these related trends, executives will be far more mobile in their career. This will have serious implications, in that executives will have to deal with a rapid turnover in the workforce.

The overriding implication of these developments is that no position can be regarded as permanent. Rapid societal change exacerbates this phenomenon. Thus temporary systems are the norm. Executives need to be aware that the only form of tenure one can get in a company is the one offered by its customers. As a result, people have to adopt a more proactive attitude toward career management. As they say at Apple, "You have to manage your own career. We provide you with the opportunities." In short, job tenure has been replaced by employability.

The need to do one's own thing will also be reflected in an increase in the number of entrepreneurs and their corollary, family businesses. The impulse toward taking control of one's personal environment, and toward managing a wider field of influence, means that ownership of a business will become an increasingly attractive option, particularly for women, who will choose entrepreneurship as a more effective way of managing both a career and family life.

The revolution in information and communication technology is changing the way people work. A vast array of information is readily available nowadays through the proliferation of computer networks. The ease with which executives can obtain this information enables them to have a greater number of people reporting directly to them. One of the implications of this is that middle management's role in processing the information flow between top management and the operating level becomes increasingly superfluous; corporate staff functions become less important. Jack Welch's vision of General Electric—a corporate structure that involves less room for middle management and staff—would be difficult to realize without the new developments in information processing. ASEA Brown Boveri (ABB) is another good example of a company that has taken advantage of developments in communication. ABB, which was formed from two power-equipment companies, one

Swedish and one Swiss, is made up of 1,300 separate companies divided into 5,000 profit centers whose structure and control depend on modern advances in information technology.

The information revolution is one of the factors enabling organizations to become flatter. Tall, hierarchical companies with many layers of management will eventually be extinct. New, flatter organizations will start to resemble a kind of subcontracting station with a central core, lots of part-time workers, and a large number of subcontractors. Lateral communication (as opposed to vertical communication) will become the rule rather than the exception. Networking will be permanent. The "decentralized centralized" structure will become the norm.

As a concomitant, decentralization itself will be more acceptable than in the past. One of the benefits of new information technology is that decentralized organizations do not have to feel threatened by the fear of losing operational control. As Percy Barnevik, the president and CEO of ABB has said, "I want this company to be simultaneously big and small, decentralized and centralized, global and local!"

The design of the new organization will be more customer-centered; responding to clients' needs will be a central theme. In consequence, performance objectives and evaluation of all activities should be linked to consumer satisfaction. I have seen too many executives so busy looking inward at the organization and playing political games that they forget their most important constituency: their customers. If you do that too long, your customers may forget you too. Thus customer and supplier contact should be maximized for everyone in the organization. It is clear that a decentralized, customer-oriented organizational design gives competitive advantages in terms of speed, flexibility, and market responsiveness.

One effect of the flatter organization is that more work has to be done in an environment that is less structured than that of traditional, hierarchical institutions. This means that the executive of the future will need a much higher level of tolerance toward uncertainty and ambiguity. This change in attitude may be one of the toughest assignments for many executives.

If the growth in the number of business schools is any indication, management is also going to become more professional. It will be more difficult to get away with a seat-of-the-pants approach to management. This does not mean that the Cartesian mode of managing is the only road to salvation. Rational analysis alone can become sterile. There will be a need to balance rational, analytical approaches with intuitive thinking processes. Executives will have to become better at picking up the weak signals. They will have to become more attuned to what psychotherapists describe as countertransference reactions. They will have to cultivate the ability to interpret the kind of feelings that can be stirred up in interpersonal situations. The emotional agenda in professional encounters is often glossed over. Excellent executives, however, pay attention to these processes, which they see as extra pieces of information.

The difficulty is that these emotional processes and reactions can be extremely elusive. It might help to ask yourself the following questions in any professional encounter: What is my immediate response? How am I reacting in dealing with this person? What is this person doing to me? When I am talking or listening, what kind of thoughts and feelings come to mind?

Even if the thoughts and feelings you uncover appear quite bizarre, it is worthwhile paying attention to them. For example, you might discover that you feel a need for control in an interaction, or you might experience a sense of rejection or boredom. Alternatively, you might experience a great need to please the other person or feel afraid of him or her.

It is worthwhile to listen with an inner ear to these questions and responses, as all such reactions carry meaning. However, executives have a notoriously underdeveloped capacity for self-reflection. Many are inclined to act first and think later. They seem reluctant to ask themselves why they act the way they do. This is in part because the myopic, action-oriented environment in which many executives operate does not encourage this kind of self-examination.

In this new, dynamic, and turbulent world, there will be increased emphasis on planned change and organizational renewal. Change will have to become a permanent phenomenon in the new corporation, and the executive of the future had better learn how to live with it.

To facilitate change, a corporate culture that fosters a continuous learning process should be created. Benchmarking inside and outside the corporation is recommended, and diversity should be encouraged.

Senior executives must be psychologically prepared to take on the role of mentor and oversee the development of the next generation of executives coming into the corporation. Some companies I know of have formalized this mentoring process: Shell, Air Liquide, Johnson & Johnson, Daimler Benz, and Stora (the latter being one of the oldest companies in the world) know what it means to institute a learning environment.

Collaboration and teamwork will be essential in getting these flatter, more professional organizations to work. Excellent companies take great trouble to avoid destructive conflict and politicization. Senior executives in the organization of tomorrow will have to assume the roles of helper and coach. They should be authoritative rather than authoritarian. As participation becomes more the rule than the exception, an authoritarian approach to management will become increasingly untenable.

Senior people should be able to build a climate of trust into the organization. Without trust, communication breaks down and learning stops. As a result, people become turf defenders, lack a helpful attitude toward other people in the organization, and fail to engage in good corporate citizenship behavior by pitching in when needed.

Creating this kind of environment will require senior executives to communicate more openly and to demonstrate their commitment. An atmosphere of trust is based on honesty, consistency, and competency. In order to create this kind of climate, it is important that senior executives show respect for their subordinates and support them when the going gets tough. Keep in mind the foolproof prescription for driving others crazy: don't trust, don't feel, don't talk about it!

Another characteristic of the companies of the future will be the emergence of self-managing teams: groups of executives who need very little guidance, given their ability for personal goal setting, their capacity to reward and criticize themselves, and their level of motivation and commitment. In companies such as Apple, Microsoft, Novo Nordisk, and W. L. Gore, these new types of practices and arrangements have already become the norm.

Finally, people will have to be increasingly attentive to stress management at work. Intercontinental travel and the ever-increasing amount of information entering the workflow put an enormous strain on the mind and body. The ideal, well-adjusted executive must know how to maintain the balance between private and organizational life and not surpass an acceptable level of personal stress tolerance, recognizing when the limits have been reached. Exceeding those limits leads to burnout.

My whirlwind view of future trends in management, supplementing some of the ideas of Peters and Waterman, raises a number of obvious points in the context of excellence. First, I cannot stress strongly enough that senior executives should avoid the temptation of megalomania: they should not try to do everything. The number of supermen and superwomen who think they know all there is to know about every kind of industry and business is happily small. People who think this way are usually deluding themselves. Excellent companies focus on only a few businesses. Research on this topic indicates that the added value provided by diversification in nonrelated industries is highly suspect.[1] Fortunately, the merger and acquisition mania of the eighties has quieted down (though, as I noted in Chapter Four, it has not spent itself); many companies, having learned a costly lesson, are now divesting and refocusing, going back to their core competencies. The Prudential Corporation, for example, has decided to concentrate once again on its main business—selling life insurance and pensions—and has divested itself of its real estate agencies, car and home insurance, and foreign subsidiaries. The Italian car giant, Fiat, has decided to pare down nonstrategic assets such as its insurance and retailing businesses. AB Skandia, after a devastating takeover battle that bankrupted two of its rivals, has likewise decided to go back to basics, while the Finnish company Nokia has sold its electrical holdings. These are examples of companies that have changed course to prepare for the future; the list is lengthy and significant.

Executive talent is a scarce resource, and it will become scarcer as more and more companies join the global game. The number of people with outstanding abilities is limited, so a company's skill at attracting stars will be crucial. As a matter of fact, this may eventually turn out to be the Achilles' heel of many Japanese companies, which favor the practice of putting only nationals in top management positions.

Another factor in the pursuit of excellence is speed, which has become a very competitive weapon. Japanese car manufacturers need only three years to produce a whole new vehicle, from planning to product launch. Can General Motors or Fiat do the same? Richard Branson, the founder of The Virgin Group, says that he can have an idea in the morning and see it implemented in the evening. His company is dancing. Can the same be said of Du Pont or France Telecom?

This brave new organizational world needs imaginative management of human resources. Obviously, the winning corporation has to offer a fair amount of job security, with high salaries reflecting the conditions of the job market. In such an organization, the traditional adversarial role of unions will be minimized. Job benefits will have to be tailored to individual needs. For example, today's young executives are likely to demand a piece of the action in the form of profit sharing, bonuses, and/or stock options. After all, we are living in the age of the gold-collar worker.

A key variable in this pursuit of excellence—particularly in technology-driven companies—is how the company manages creativity and innovation, and in this context there are a number of things to be said. In the first place, innovation costs money. Innovative companies such as Merck, Compaq, Motorola, and Johnson & Johnson spend a considerable amount of money on research and development.

The amount varies, of course, but the general figure is around 10 percent. A considerable proportion of this research money should be spent on new products. Companies such as 3M and Rubbermaid try to ensure that at least 25 to 30 percent of their sales comes from products generated within the preceding five years.

To make such a level of innovation possible, these companies allow their researchers an exceptional degree of freedom. For example, both Hewlett-Packard and 3M have "bootlegging" percentage rules that specify a particular percentage of time that researchers are encouraged to spend on their pet projects.

This sort of innovative organization makes the best facilities and equipment available to its researchers. Ideally, it tries to create a kind of college campus atmosphere within the company. To promote synergy, it also constructs a substantial interface between academia and the organization through seminars, joint research projects, and other forms of collaboration.

The key word here is *flexibility*. Paperwork has to be minimized; otherwise, creative people are not going to stick around. Money and space for exploratory work should be made readily available, and senior executives should allow innovative researchers the freedom to fail. The organization has to tolerate mistakes and not interfere. The eleventh commandment at 3M is this: "Thou shalt not kill a new product idea." As one of the senior executives at 3M once said, "At times we have to walk around with our eyes half closed, trying to keep our mouth shut."

This is not to say that hands-on involvement of the CEO in product development is not extremely important. It is, especially if a CEO has expertise in a particular area. For example, Roy Vagelos, former chairman of the pharmaceutical company Merck (which has been listed year after year in *Fortune* as one of the most successful companies, if not the most successful company, in the United States), had a background as a medical doctor and head of the biological chemistry department at Washington University. Vagelos, who had a very good idea of what his scientists were talking about, was definitely not merely an auditor of financial reports.

Life in innovative organizations is like a sports event where different units are engaged in friendly competition. Nothing gets the adrenaline going as much as healthy rivalry. Apart from the financial rewards, there are many other prizes available to those who are successful. For example, at Merck the ultimate accolade is the Scientific Award of the Board of Directors, which includes a grant of $50,000 to be donated to a university of the winner's choice.

Product champions play a key role in innovative organizations. But given the political nature of organizations, even champions need protectors to help make their ideas a reality. They need executive sponsors who, as the 3M executive quoted earlier implied, should be slightly blind, deaf, and dumb, highly tolerant of their innovators' ideas. New ideas are extremely delicate flowers; they quickly wilt. Differences in opinion should be encouraged. After all, when we all think alike, nobody is thinking. Moreover, one's ability to perform competently decreases in proportion to the number of people watching.

If product champions are successful in bringing their ideas to fruition, they should also be given the opportunity to manage their new products. That makes for a sense of ownership and increases commitment and motivation.

In general, in companies where excellence is determined by technological innovation, two different career tracks may be needed: one management and one scientific. A person should have the choice of refusing promotion into the management track without being financially penalized. The mistake of turning an excellent scientist into a lousy manager should be avoided at all cost.

Obviously, in customer-oriented organizations, close collaboration is needed between marketing people and people at the research lab, and the same is true for people in product development and manufacturing design. Equally, customers should be involved at an early stage in new product development and in the improvement of existing products.

Finally, the executive engaged in pursuit of the elusive quality of excellence has to be something of a tightrope walker. To keep all the various demands of the different stakeholders in equilibrium is not easy, even if the executive can overcome a fear of heights. But consider the alternative. Who wants to go voluntarily to the corporate graveyard? Those in pursuit of excellence should never forget that the two most difficult things to handle in life are failure and success. The challenge of handling failure is understandable, of course. However, it is less obvious that a surfeit of success, which leads to arrogance and complacency, can itself cause failure.

Part II

. . . .

Leaders and Individuals

Sherlock Holmes once told Dr. Watson, "You see, but you don't observe," but the famous detective did not find it easy to explain to his sidekick how these two ways of looking at things diverge. At times, in taking the reader on the organizational journey that makes up this book, I have also tried to show the difference between seeing and observing. Readers will discover, after taking a closer look, that the answer to many organizational riddles lies under their nose. Again, it is useful to quote Sherlock Holmes: "It has long been an axiom of mine that the little things are infinitely the most important." The only problem is that most of us are not like Sherlock Holmes. We have to learn *how* to look and *where* to look.

To illustrate, not very long ago, I was doing a workshop in a little town in Portugal. The organizers, quite market-driven, had probably been too optimistic in listing all the benefits that participants would instantly derive from my workshop. If one had believed the publicity (which was translated for me only afterward), one would have thought that by the end of our time together, the participants would know all the secrets of leadership. Not only would they understand everything about their own leadership style, but their newly acquired knowledge would make everyone around them completely transparent. They would be able to see straight through other people and figure out what made them tick. It sounded like the ultimate power trip: gaining the ability to make anybody do what they wanted done. Obviously, the people who had signed up for the workshop were looking for magic; they were in search of a quick fix.

After a reasonably productive first morning, during which I talked about some of the darker aspects of leadership, I began to sense some impatience. The participants were discovering that I was a poor snake-oil salesman; the expected magical tools were not forthcoming. Only a few concepts that centered around leadership, applicable or not to their own situation, were being presented.

One of the participants, who was much more assertive than the others, asked me what I was attempting to do. He told me straight out that he was getting lost. Where was I going? When I repeated once more my agenda for the two-day workshop, he declared that he had no interest at all in topics such as corporate culture, national culture, succession planning, entrepreneurship, or family business. He made it quite clear that what he was really interested in was himself. He wanted me to be the mirror, telling him everything about his personal style, his strengths and weaknesses, and how he could become more effective. Obviously, his was a very laudable request—but a little bit difficult to execute on the spot.

My initial reaction was surprise. I was doing a seminar similar to the kind I had done many times before, usually with very good results. I experienced his rather aggressive way of confronting me as an assault. On one level, I was making an effort to understand logically what was going on. On another, more experiential level, I was trying to make sense of his aggressive attitude. What was this person trying to do to me?

Intrigued, and ready to do something quite different, I took up his challenge. In light of his request, I asked him if he would be willing to be a life case study. Without hesitation, he accepted, and after some prompting proceeded to talk quite frankly about his life in general and his career in particular. It quickly became clear that his abrasiveness had become his Achilles' heel. Until recently, he had been able to get away with an abrasive manner, but lately it had become more problematic. In fact, it was this that had brought him to the seminar. His boss (the president of his company) had strongly suggested that some kind of leadership seminar would be a good experience for him.

It became clear from this man's presentation (in spite of his attempts at evasion) that he had recently been demoted. After having had responsibility for the largest unit in the company, he had been given the leadership of a small staff group. This was not the only serious setback he had had to deal with, however. In addition, he had recently received feedback from a yearly organizational climate survey done at his company, and that feedback showed that although his people respected him as a competent, achievement-oriented manager, they also compared him to Genghis Khan in terms of abrasiveness.

Listening to his life history, I did not find it difficult to find the red thread that explained some of his behavior. It became clear that his parents had assigned him the mission of making up for the disappointments they had experienced themselves. He was expected to set their world right. His father had been at the receiving end of a very poor deal instigated by a number of relatives, necessitating a new start in life at a very late age. His mother had always emphasized to him that nice guys finish last (which, she would say, is what had happened to his father). The repetitive message given to him was that it was a very dangerous world out there; most people could not be trusted. The proof was in the unfair way his father had been treated: people had run circles around him and stabbed him in the back.

With this kind of indoctrination, the participant's particular philosophy of life did not come as a great surprise. According to the script that predominated in his inner theater, in interacting with others it was much better to go right for the jugular. Subtlety was excess baggage. Straight shooting, even if it hurt, was preferable. In addition, it was also advisable not to be too trusting.

This life strategy had paid off well in his former role as a turnaround manager. In that position, he could not be delicate about other people's feelings. And even earlier in his career, when he had served in a technical position that necessitated only limited inter-face with other people, his abrasiveness had been less noticeable. But now that he was at the head office, having been tapped as the crown prince as a reward for work well done, it was obvious that his personal style had become a problem.

Given the pain he was in (his marriage was also in poor shape), this particular person was willing to listen to some of the advice given by me and the other seminar participants during his presen-tation. My initial emotional reaction, the experience of being attacked, helped me in making my opening interpretations. This way of relating to others was the essence of his interpersonal style. I felt that I had to metabolize his aggressiveness somehow. But his abrasiveness had aroused anger in me. This anger and my sense that I was being treated unfairly (just as he felt he had been treated unfairly—as a proxy for his father—throughout his life) were give-away indications of the major themes that preoccupied his inner world. By reflecting on the emotions this man aroused in me, I had avoided the trap of a knee-jerk response. I had not merely reacted to his abrasiveness; I had tried to understand it and to utilize the weak signals he was giving me to help him in his predicament.

There are many ways of describing what happened. Call it coun-tertransference, projective identification, or parallel processes, if you will. The importance lies not in the name but in the acknowledg-ment of the process, of the kind of impact certain individuals have on others. People have the tendency to introject into others what they are experiencing themselves, and that serves as another source of information in understanding the person.

As this example illustrates, in my efforts to demystify issues throughout this book, my magnifying glass has been a clinical ori-entation to organizational analysis. And in reading the different essays, you will discover that the basic principles that make up the clinical paradigm are not necessarily complex. It is often a question only of recognizing their applicability—taking note of one's per-sonal reactions—to many different situations.

A major part of organizational life comes out in these stories told by the organizational participants. As organizational analysts, our task is to interpret these stories correctly. And the explorer of this terrain will quickly discover that it is not necessarily the historical truth that matters. On the contrary, it is the narrative truth, the emotional experience remembered by the storyteller.

Only by actively reviewing how these stories are experienced by both narrator and receiver will we find the real person behind them and recognize both how these stories influence behavior and action and how they can lead to "neurotic" organizations. To make this understanding possible (as we have seen in the previous example), we have to figure out the themes that dominate the lives of the principal raconteurs in the organization. We have to understand the character of these people. We have to see the persons behind the mask. As the psychiatrist Robert Coles once said, "Character is how you behave in response to the company you keep, seen and unseen." And the unseen is the most difficult part to decipher.

Of course, helping executives understand how their behavior affects their company is not the same as psychoanalyzing companies. Putting organizations on the couch basically means using clinical conceptualizations in order to understand better what really goes on in organizations. The next essays touch on a wide range of the human dilemmas I have observed in leaders.

Chapter Ten opens Pandora's box and looks at how physiological and psychological processes differ according to gender, addressing the stereotypes as well as the realities that arise from these differences in the organizational context.

In Chapter Eleven, another difficult set of issues is addressed: the tension and stress that can unbalance innovative and successful family firms. Questions of succession and management style are frequently at the bottom of bitter conflict and can lead to the downfall of the company. These problems are intensified when the personal relations between family members spill over into their business. This chapter gives pragmatic advice for both owners and employees of family firms.

One of the most frequently cited positive aspects of family firms is their energy and creativity. Although it may seem to be a Sisyphean task, attaining creativity is something that any organization—even the most hidebound—can achieve. On the other hand, if creativity is not managed properly, it can result in chaos. Chapter Twelve looks at what differentiates truly creative people from common mortals and examines how to acquire and nurture them in organizations.

In order to understand human behavior, it is necessary to realize that subconscious processes determine the way individuals act and make decisions. The next set of essays examines the darker side of leadership and some of the reasons behind dysfunctional leadership traits.

Chapter Thirteen is an account of a traumatic period in any leader's career: retirement and succession. Why is it literally life-threatening for some, while for others it is just another rite of passage in a full and rewarding life? What can be done to facilitate this type of change, both from an individual and an organizational perspective?

Workaholism is another common type of dysfunctional behavior. Early childhood experience can cause individuals to internalize a set of harsh and unrealistic expectations for their own behavior that are carried into adulthood. Hard work is a form of redemption, but it is never quite enough. Chapter Fourteen shows ways in which workaholic behavior can be changed.

We can find other people in organizations who can be named *alexithymics*. Alexithymia, meaning literally "no words for emotions," describes individuals who show no emotion (and in fact seem to *feel* no emotion). These individuals are often to be found in large organizations, where they can hide behind structure and routine. Alexithymic leaders can infect their organizations. At the very least, as Chapter Fifteen shows, they are likely to lack the charismatic, energizing qualities that are essential to effective leadership.

Many dysfunctional characteristics of leadership originate in an unhealthy type of narcissism, a reaction against feelings of insignificance. Chapter Sixteen discusses how entrepreneurs are prone to this type of reaction, which in turn fuels their drive to succeed despite the forces they believe are aligned against them. Robert Maxwell is a recent example of an entrepreneur with a dark side.

How can leaders such as Robert Maxwell remain successful and powerful for so long given their aggressive and irrational behavior? Why would anyone want to work for such leaders? To get at the answer, consider the fact that excess is the trademark not only of some leaders but also of some followers. Chapter Seventeen studies the strange phenomena of excessive submissive behavior and folie à deux and shows how attachment to a leader can become so intense that it overwhelms followers' abilities to think and act rationally, often to their own detriment.

Some leaders go beyond even the dysfunctional kinds of behavior we have looked at up to now. They seem to go mad; there is no longer any observable rationale to explain their actions. Chapter Eighteen begins with an account of Saddam Hussein, a leader who has undeniable charisma, but charisma tinged with madness. What are some of the key factors that push a leader over the edge? Once again we find that the answer lies in the double-edged sword of narcissism. Narcissism can be a positive, constructive force, or it can turn into the foundation for an excess of hubris and irrational thinking.

Though diverse in nature, the essays in Part Two share a common thread: the underlying dynamics of an individual executive's problems—his or her core conflictual relationship themes—and how they affect the organization. By facing these themes, the reader will become aware that certain problems are deeply rooted and cannot be resolved merely by introducing a new planning system, changing appraisal and reward systems, writing up new job descriptions, or tinkering with the organization's design. Frequently, at the core of these difficulties are people problems. And to change these takes a much greater effort. The reader does well to realize that it is essential to look beyond external factors and be aware of the fact that in organizational change and development, there is no such thing as a quick fix. Leaders in particular need to understand the extent to which they, and ultimately their organization, are influenced by their own inner theater.

· ·

Is Anatomy Really Destiny?

Women as Leaders

> *I can feel for her because, although I have never been*
> *an Alaskan prostitute dancing on a bar in a spangled*
> *dress, I still get very bored with washing and ironing*
> *and dishwashing and cooking day after relentless day.*
>
> Betty MacDonald

This essay is about a group of potential leaders that is often over-looked or underestimated. This group is made up of about half of the working population. Yes, you guessed it: I am talking about women. As numerous articles in such magazines as *Fortune*, *Forbes*, and *Business Week* have pointed out, in spite of all the initiatives and legislation, in spite of contraception and feminism, women are still extraordinarily scarce in senior management.

Personally, I find a good indicator of this sorry state of affairs in the number of women enrolled in the programs at INSEAD. In the Advanced Management Program, I count myself lucky if I find two or three women in a group of 150 men. This clearly demonstrates that senior management is still very much an all-male preserve.

Fortune found that in the largest public corporations in the United States, women hold less than 0.5 percent of the highest-paid management jobs. The situation is certainly not any better in Europe, to say nothing about Japan.[1] Fortunately, there seems to be some change afoot. This year in my MBA classes, for example, 19 percent of the students are women (admittedly still a far cry from the numbers found in U.S. business schools, where women fall more in the 30 to 40 percent range).

Why do we find such a small percentage of women in the higher echelons of management? Was Freud right when he said that anatomy is destiny? What are the reasons for these low numbers?

People willing to speculate about this state of affairs are numerous. They come up with a whole potpourri of arguments: women do not have the same drive as men; women do not look at their work as a career but as a series of jobs; women's emotionalism blocks their way up; the family is more important to women than their job; women are not part of the old-boy network; women have a harder time finding mentors.

Many of these arguments illustrate the persistence of stereotypes. In fact, if we take the line of thought they represent to its absurd conclusion, the result is something like this: men in organizations are logical, rational, aggressive, competitive, and independent—they are the ones with the right stuff, the real leadership abilities—while women, given their "natural" social role, are more intuitive, emotional, docile, cooperative, and nurturing, and thus they are obviously far more suited for the role of follower!

It is high time to look at the situation differently: instead of being impeded by stereotypes, we would find it far more constructive to look at stereotypes from a more clinical angle and find out if there is some truth in them. Do women really behave different than men? And if they do, why?

One interesting study that provides some answers to these questions was done a number of years ago by Carol Gilligan of the Harvard School of Education. The basic argument of her book *In a Different Voice* is that women have a more nurturing nature than men—not a great surprise to most of us. The question remains why?

Like other psychologists before her, Gilligan states that basic gender identity for girls comes from experiencing themselves as their mothers. On their part, adult women fear separateness and consequently make a greater effort to keep relationships going. This is in contrast with boys, whose basic gender identity is determined by being the exact opposite of their mothers. Obviously, it is important for men to make a clear break with their mothers in order to prove their separateness. The psychological end result is that men are not as comfortable with intimacy; they are easily threatened by it.

The development of women's interpersonal skills tends to start very early in life. The girl, if she wants eventually to have "normal," heterosexual relationships, needs to shift her attention from the original "object"—the mother—to the father. But her relationship with her mother, given their physical similarity, is too important merely to break off. Consequently, girls develop from early on a greater talent for transforming their relationships with their mother and father. Obviously, the boy does not have this dilemma, since in the case of normal sexual development, the original object of affection remains the mother, who is the representation of all later female figures. From these early developments, interpersonal sensitivity, empathy, sharing, and helping take on a more central position in a woman's inner world.

Given the human need to establish a sexual identity, we can see how differences in behavior patterns in men and women have something to do with the way boys and girls resolve their relationships with their parents. The challenge of separation is resolved quite differently for the two sexes: boys and girls use the forces of opposition and identification in very distinctive ways while exploring the differences and similarities of their gender.

Of course, one important element adding to gender differentiation is women's ability to do something that men cannot—that is, give birth. Besides the actual delivery of a child, this includes the whole preparation for it—awareness of the biological clock and pregnancy, with all its bodily changes—and the subsequent feeding and nurturing of children.

These special physiological processes, along with their unique version of gender identity formation, imply that nurturance and relationship maintenance are necessarily central for women. As a matter of fact, some women in the business world may be so preoccupied with keeping relationships going that they find themselves clear off the road to the executive suite. They may be so busy responding to nonverbal cues and mood states that the digestion of more factual information suffers. Men, on the other hand, can be oblivious to relational and nonverbal information—relationships be damned! And unfortunately, given the male-dominated business culture we live in, they can get away with it. The kudos all too often go to those who are more factually inclined.

As if there were not enough problems for a single working woman, becoming part of a dual-career family complicates the matter even further. Here the key words are *overload* and *stress*. Many women do not have a very easy time juggling multiple roles: they strive to be not only an ideal career woman but an exemplary mother and wife as well.

Adding to the normal stress at work, women are victimized by the fact that a remarkable number of male executives are still very uncomfortable with women colleagues. What adds insult to injury is that many women are exposed to some form of sexual harassment at one time or another. Like it or not, the sexual dimension is ever-present.

Perhaps an underlying reason for men's discomfort at having women in senior positions has something to do with the "flight from mother." Let me explain what I mean by this. Mothers are usually the first nurturers and consequently the first powerholders. They have the power to withhold food and to punish. (By the way, this need on the part of some women to exert domination and control in nurturing can be seen as a reaction to a lack of power in other areas.) This helpless dependence may give rise to strong feelings of rage, envy, fear, and shame on the part of the child. Not only may these early feelings contribute to a later need not to find oneself in a similar position; in the case of boys, they may contribute to an inclination to devalue the woman. How can you be envious of someone you look down upon? Another way of dealing with such feelings is to see women as merely sexual objects. Furthermore, because males have been pushed around by their mother, they do not mind pushing around a female secretary!

The view of women as threatening, engulfing entities (again, remember that this is not necessarily a conscious process) is reflected in men's dreams and fantasies about phallic women, witches, and spider women. Psychoanalysts hypothesize that people in general yearn for that state of original closeness and attachment that they once had with their mother when they were babies. Women satisfy this need by giving birth to children, a process reinforced by subsequent nursing and feeding activities. For men, who cannot have that experience, the unsatisfied desire lingers on. At the same time, however, this longing for fusion is accompanied by a fear of losing their sense of separateness and masculine identity. Thus, deep down, men resent their unconscious dependence on women.

Moreover, for women, giving birth is one form of creative activity. The creative endeavors of men, who do not have the option of childbearing, tend to be much more centered around work; work becomes more of a narcissistic investment. For many men, it becomes the center of their being. The importance of work to men's self-esteem adds to their ambivalent attitude toward women. As a result of these factors, women's "intrusion" into the workplace is resented. Unconsciously, men may tell themselves that women have no place there (since women already have certain advantages men can never have). Men want women as admirers, not competitors. Consequently, it can be said that men tend to feel more comfortable with men, while women feel comfortable with both men and women.

But there is even more to say about men's and women's intrapsychic theater: women can become prisoners of their own stereotypes as to what is proper behavior in their relationships with husband and children. Are traditional mothers the ideal? You may think so. Of course, such mothering has its advantages, and most children appreciate having a mother around all the time. However, women who have experienced and valued a cozy childhood with the consistent presence of a nurturing mother may, if they should choose later on to mother their children differently, pay the high price of guilt.

The social stereotypes of what a mother should be reinforce women's feelings of guilt vis-à-vis their children. Mothers tend to feel more responsibility for the continuing success and happiness of their offspring than do fathers. When something goes wrong, they are the first to be blamed—even by themselves.

A woman may also feel guilty in regard to her husband. Maybe he married her thinking she would be like her mother, she thinks. But the demands of a woman's job can often become greater than she or he would really like. Her dilemma then becomes whether or not she can live up to his fantasies of what a woman should be like. (Remember, she knows that his own mother served as a role model. Poor guy: there is even less of a chance that she will be like *his* mother!)

Added to these pressures is a conflict in roles. At work a woman is supposed to be competitive, an achiever. In contrast, at home she is supposed to be caring, a nurturer. What if she should become confused, put on the wrong hat and behave inappropriately?

Some women begin to worry that they are becoming what they perceive as too successful. It may be that they have never really overcome stereotypes about their gender that define women as less competent than men. Consequently, some successful women feel like impostors. In their heart of hearts, they cannot believe that they did it themselves—that their efforts and their efforts alone created their success.

Others worry that too much success will interfere in their relationships with men. They might be accused of having lost their femininity by men (or by other women) who feel threatened by women's success, for example. The result can be that they become their own worst enemies, holding themselves back as far as career advancement is concerned. As a recourse, these women may start engaging in self-defeating acts, demonstrating that they really are quite helpless; they cannot reach a higher position.

The feeling that men might become envious is not a mere fantasy. There *are* men who have a very hard time when their partner becomes too successful. It's all right with them when the little woman does something to keep herself busy, but when she starts moving up the corporate ladder, these men perceive this success as a personal affront to their masculinity. Symbolically, they perceive it as a sign of their not being man enough to take care of the family.

Most women in business find that having it all—at least having it all at once—is not an easy task. How can women have the same chances as men to find time both to play and to enjoy work to its fullest? Making more time by giving up sleep is not the answer. And trying to do it all can lead to burnout symptoms, such as feelings of powerlessness, dependency reactions (which may be accompanied by eating, drinking, or smoking disorders or drug abuse), denial, or depression.

Where does this all lead, and what can be done about it? What are the options? Certain women among those who choose or have to work have come to the conclusion that having a career is not so important; it is not their ambition to reach the top. (Of course, that can be a rationalization.) They prefer to find jobs with a flexible schedule in order to juggle better the demands of work and home.

Other women—those who are ambitious in their career—want to have it all (like men). They want to have both a career and a family life and say that they are prepared to make the sacrifices that go with that choice. There is a catch: if a woman wants to be a fast-track executive, it is very hard to have children, in spite of the possible good intentions of her husband to share family duties. Many husbands seem to be good as cheerleaders, but that is where their involvement stops. When it comes down to it, they do very few chores at home. Although times are changing, how many men, in their heart of hearts, are comfortable with the role of househusband?

One possibility for women who want both a career and children is that of paid help. The problem with this solution is that the parents have to decide whether they really want their child raised by a series of housekeepers or nannies. The dilemma for many women is the knowledge that the first three years of life are critical in the formation of personality. Even after that, when the children can fend for themselves, what are the emotional implications of being latchkey children—children who have to manage on their own after school until the parents come home? And what about the TV as baby-sitter?

We have not heard the last word about working parents' child-rearing practices and their implications for children. Is the argument that it is quality time that really matters a copout? Maybe so. How can we tell? Which is the better alternative: to have the child raised by an angry, frustrated, homebound mother or by a mother who has already put in a long hard day at work?

Some women choose a mixed option: a fast track early in the career cycle (during which the career is established), followed by a period when family life becomes more important (while offspring are infants and young children), and then a return to the working world. The drawback of such a choice is that the woman will be far behind her male peers during the third period; she will be out of phase on the career trajectory. However well it is timed, a pregnancy is difficult to fit into today's male-oriented career timetable.

It is interesting to note, however, that women who go back to work later in life are often more pleased with what they are doing than men of their age range, many of whom have gone or are going through the infamous midlife crisis. Apart from many other pressures on men, during this period the notion that organizations are funnels really hits home. Men discover that there is not much room at the top, and they have to work through the disappointment involved. Even for those men who avoid a full-scale crisis, a sense of burnout is not uncommon at this stage in the career cycle. In contrast, women entering the workforce anew are usually in a much better state of mind and are full of energy and hope. They do not generally suffer from the kind of burnout experienced by men. As I have observed all too often, there are an enormous number of managers who behave at work like sleepwalkers.

Some women are interested in a career but not in joining the ranks of corporate management. They have come to the conclusion that being in such positions does not give them enough flexibility. These women solve the problem by striking off on their own. Women are taking that option with a vengeance. In the United States, women are now starting new enterprises at a rate three times that of men. They own more than a quarter of the country's sole proprietorships. Women in Europe are not far behind. Probably one of the most famous success stories is that of Anita Roddick and the Body Shop. Her company, one of the most profitable young firms on the London stock exchange, is now operating in thirty-seven countries. Another woman operating in the retail trade is Sonia Rykiel. Her empire, which is built on her signature clothing, now has a turnover of about $70 million, with 47 boutiques and 550 points of sale in 36 countries.

Anita Roddick and Sonia Rykiel are as yet exceptions. Most of the new companies stay small. The women are not out there to build an empire; they want to support themselves. These women have left the "mommy track" behind. They have decided to go back into the workforce after raising their kids or divorcing. They want a flexible schedule and the opportunity to work at home. They want to create a new balance in their lives. Small entrepreneurial businesses are the natural outcome of these needs.

So where does all this bring us? What is the portrait of the modern businesswoman? A woman's background can be a key factor in her development as a successful career woman. Based on the limited sample of women with whom I have worked and consulted, I have found that there are more female high achievers in families where there are no sons or where sons are in the minority. Because they had less competition growing up, these women may have developed a privileged relationship with their father, who had high expectations for the daughter. Because of the composition of the family, these women were subjected to less social stereotyping. (Of course, the whole family constellation is changing with more women entering higher management positions and becoming new role models.)

Women who develop a greater awareness of their own capabilities will do better in the workplace. (This is of course true for men as well.) What is particularly important is knowing how to set priorities and having the capacity to say no without feeling guilty. Sticking to the "little girl" gender role and waiting for men to take the lead is not a good idea, although it does not hurt to ask for help when in trouble. There is no need to act out the role of the lonely cowgirl. Finding a supportive mentor can be a great help in this process.

Actually, one of the reasons women get into trouble in the workplace is that they have more difficulty than men in delegating. After all, good girls take orders; they do not give them. Women are not as verbally assertive as men in business meetings, nor do they promote themselves as men do. The time has come, however, to change the scenario. Women should learn how to be more assertive and competitive, which does not have to mean losing one's femininity. Because there are many different ways of saying something assertively, women simply have to choose the one that suits their style.

Of course, businesses should help carry the burden. Providing financially or otherwise for day-care centers or child-care referral services is a great start. Having an on-site day-care center is an even greater help (but this is an expensive option and thus as yet not a priority for male-dominated executive boards). The importance of the structure of maternity and parental leave benefits should not be underestimated. Flextime, part-time employment, and job sharing are other creative ways of helping women at work. I realize, however, that these latter arrangements are usually more workable for lower-level executives.

Given the trend toward flatter organizations, with their emphasis on coaching, teamwork, power and information sharing, and networking, women's talents in these areas (which are due to their greater mastery of interpersonal skills) will work to their advantage. As a matter of fact, the types of organization now emerging seem to be tailored toward the skills of women. The challenge ahead for women is to find the right balance between such polarities as toughness and femininity, competitiveness and care, and facts and feelings. In so doing, women will profoundly change the existing business culture and bring into being more humane and more creative organizations.

. . . .

Joining the Family Burlesque
Family Firms

When my father died . . . six weeks after making me
head of [the company]—I was the most frightened
man in America. . . . Not a day went by when I
didn't think about the old boy, but the only thing
I really worried about was lousing the business up. . . .

I had a ritual I used to follow on the anniversary
of my father's death. I would spend a quiet evening
taking stock of what [the company] had accomplished
in his absence, and then say to [my wife], "That's
another year I've made it alone."[1]

Thomas Watson, Jr.

More and more women and men are making the decision to break out of the mold and form their own company. These family firms are often exemplary organizations, flexible and innovative, particularly while the entrepreneur is still at the top. However, it is essential not to overlook the enormous emotional burdens that come with working in a family firm. The man who described in the above epigraph his reaction to taking over the family firm had certainly not forgotten his father (a famous and gifted entrepreneur). The father haunted him like the figure of the *Commandatore* haunts Don Juan in Mozart's opera. His brief anecdote exemplifies the lasting influence a powerful individual can have on an organization. In family firms, the ghosts seem to be exceptionally active.

Many studies show that tension and stress are rampant in family firms.[2] Father-son conflicts in particular can be unusually intense. Questions of succession and appropriate management style are the issues that most frequently spark conflict. Many family firms seem to bear out comedian George Burns's assertion that "happiness is having a large, loving, caring, close-knit family in another city."

The epigraph that opens this chapter is taken from the autobiography of Thomas Watson, Jr., son of the founder of IBM. His book, *Father, Son, & Co.: My Life at IBM and Beyond*, makes it quite clear that IBM was run like a family firm for almost six decades (although, paradoxically, the Watson family never owned more than 5 percent of its stock).

Some of you may protest that it is not accurate to call IBM a family firm. Indeed, much depends on the way that a family business is defined. A conservative definition is an entity whose majority ownership or control lies within a single family and whose management involves two or more family members. A broader definition, however, is a firm in which the owner's family has a significant impact on strategic direction and on the appointment of the CEO. IBM under the Watsons would certainly fit the latter definition.

It is often wrongly assumed that family firms are a thing of the past, gone the way of the butcher, the baker, and the candlestick maker. A look at the figures, however, shows otherwise. It is estimated that 70 to 90 percent of all businesses are family-controlled, both in the United States (where 175 of the Fortune 500 companies are family-owned) and in Europe. It is also worth mentioning that family-owned businesses in the United States employ half the workforce and produce around 40 percent of the gross national product.[3]

Good (if surprising) news so far. But now for the bad news. Only three out of every ten family firms will last through to the second generation, and only one in ten will make it through to the third. The average life span of an entrepreneurial firm is twenty-four years—generally the length of time that the founder is associated with it.[4] Obviously, there is a lot of *Sturm und Drang* in a family firm. Thus it is not unusual for a family to go from rags to riches to rags again in three generations.

What are some of the common problems to be found in family firms? Let us look first at one of the most emotional issues: nepotism. Because it is more the rule than the exception that family politics overrules business logic in family-owned concerns, nepotism is inevitable and cannot be ignored. All too often, family members are welcomed into the firm on the basis of family considerations rather than their ability to contribute. The same thing can be said for advancement. Family firms can show an extraordinary tolerance for incompetent family members. Predictably, such management practices fail to impart feelings of equality and belonging to non–family members. This, combined with autocratic, paternalistic management practices, may make it hard to attract capable executives. Even worse, the people who decide to stay on may be exactly the kind one does not want in any company: yea-sayers.

Family members can also put a lot of financial strain on the company if people begin milking the business. Likewise, questions of equity and fair treatment are raised if family members are rewarded according to need rather than performance: John may be useless, but he has ten children; so shouldn't he have a higher salary than Peter, even though Peter really pulls his weight?

This imbalance between contribution and compensation brings me to something I like to call the "spoiled kid syndrome." This phenomenon is typical among children of company founders, among whom a certain type of scenario seems to repeat itself. The principal actor (most often a man) is a hardworking entrepreneur completely obsessed by the business he founded. He works night and day, neglecting his wife and children in the process. He rationalizes his neglect of his family by telling himself that everyone will be better off in the long run. However, this sort of behavior carries a heavy penalty in terms of the guilt he feels. One way of dealing with these feelings is to bribe the members of the family with material gifts to compensate for physical and emotional unavailability. First it may be a teddy bear, later an expensive trip abroad, then a sports car or condominium on the Riviera. But attractive as these gifts may be, such gestures do not make up for the attention that his children missed when young. Children bribed in this way frequently fail to acquire a sense of the value of work and personal accomplishment. This may be reflected in the way they relate to the family business and the other employees. They may turn out to be highly ineffective executives who run the company into the ground.

Another consequence of the emotional unavailability of a parent is that children fight for the little quality time that is available. The envy and jealousy generated during childhood do not just go away; they linger on, to be reenacted in a business setting. Consequently, I have found myself in the unpleasant situation of seeing adult family members behaving like five-year-olds. An inherent danger of family firms is that they can keep their employees in a permanently regressed state. Family members tend to treat the firm as a "transitional object," a safe zone that buffers them from the cruel real world. But this sort of security comes at a high price. As a consultant, I have frequently found myself in the middle of screaming sessions and even fistfights. The Wars of the Roses are still being fought in a substantial number of family businesses. It is easy to see how family and business disputes can spill over on to each other.

Life in family firms at times resembles a soap opera taking on the mantle of Greek tragedy. King Laius, Jocasta, Medea, and Oedipus are regular guest stars in the family cast. As we learned from Thomas Watson, Jr., the life of the son of an entrepreneur is not necessarily a bed of roses. Many entrepreneurs tend to be overbearing fathers. Under these circumstances, it is not always easy for a child to develop a solid sense of self-esteem. Thus sons of entrepreneurs can have a very hard time. There is even an organization in the United States that was originally called SOB, an acronym that stands for Sons of Businessmen.[5] It can best be described as a sort of

Alcoholics Anonymous, except that the participants in SOB discuss their relationship with their father rather than problems with
alcohol.

From a clinical point of view, it can be said that many entrepreneurs seem to have experienced a symbolic Oedipal victory over
their father, in that, while growing up, they gained the major por-
tion of their mother's love and affection. They will not allow a similar victory for their own son(s), however. Consequently, quite a few
have the tendency to belittle their sons, to continually put them
down. A cursory glance at business history reveals many examples
of such behavior: the first Henry Ford and his son Edsel and the
Watsons of IBM are well-known examples among many.

Naturally, problems in father-offspring relationships manifest
themselves particularly when succession is an issue. Entrepreneurs
do not easily let go. The company is too much a part of their inner
world and a symbol of who they are. They do not really trust anybody to respect their legacy; they do not intend to end up like King
Lear. Many entrepreneurs may suspect that life would be much better if they were not only immortal but free of any family attachments. But these are pipe dreams. Unfortunately, all too often
succession problems are resolved only after the entrepreneur's death.

Female entrepreneurs appear to come from a somewhat different background. As with most entrepreneurs, a major theme in their
internal theater is the wish to be in charge of their own life, to be
independent. But for women, this wish is often seen in the context
of a reaction against an unreliable father (toward whom the daughter may nevertheless maintain a feeling of special relationship) and
a submissive mother (who may have been used as a doormat by the
father). Coco Chanel came from this sort of background. She vowed
that she would never find herself in her mother's situation; she was
not going to be dependent on anybody.

Another, more positive scenario out of which the female entrepreneur appears is a family where the father strongly supports his
daughter (perhaps secretly wishing for a son and encouraging her

to be a tomboy) and where there are a number of strong female role models in the family.

Interestingly, father-daughter associations usually work out rather better than father-son relationships in business. Frequently, male entrepreneurs find it easier to relate to their daughters. Despite this, many of them have a rather traditional view of the role of women and do not prepare their daughters as possible successors. This is changing, however, and we can expect a greater number of female presidents in family enterprises in the future. As far as the children of female entrepreneurs are concerned, the data are unfortunately insufficient to surmise whether the eventual outcome of these relationships will also be a soap opera. I hypothesize, however, that the outcome will be less dramatic than is the case with many male entrepreneurs, given the fact that work seems to be more important to men than women in the formation of self-esteem and identity.

When one looks at the reasons underlying the behavior of members of family firms, it is possible to tease out a number of myths. For example, a common myth I have encountered is the fantasy of togetherness: the Myth of Harmony. In spite of all the evidence to the contrary, and notwithstanding the fact that there is an enormous amount of conflict and tension in the family, the principals prefer to ignore the reality of the situation through denial and idealization. Facts are ignored; history is rewritten. This way of dealing with reality—or rather, *not* dealing with it—originates in the outlook that the world is basically a dangerous place, so it is safer to stick together and not rock the boat.

Another common myth is the Myth of Stereotyping, in which everyone in the family has been assigned a specific role. This is based on the expectation that if certain behavioral boundaries are crossed, catastrophe will follow. As a result, all family members are tied to specific roles and consequently are stuck in specific jobs. There is no flexibility, no possibility of trying something new. Preconceptions dating from childhood predetermine adult opportunities: Johnny is not put in charge of sales, even though he might be rather good at that job, because he is not strong and should not travel (he was a sickly child); Father should be spared certain types of information since he has a weak heart—and so on.

Another very common myth is the Myth of Martyrdom. Martyrs make a big deal about doing things against their will. Despite the power they hold, they maintain that they have no choice or control. A good example of this is the owner of a company—again, usually a male—who never stops protesting that he does not really like working such long hours but is obliged to do so in order to provide for his family. This person will not admit that there are other ways to go about the work, that he does not have to put in such long hours, that he could delegate more. He cannot acknowledge that he acts the way he does simply because he *enjoys* it. He *likes* to be at the office, exerting control. As Sam Steinberg, the late owner-manager of what was once the largest grocery store chain in Canada, used to say, "I don't have ulcers; I give ulcers."

Then there is the Myth of the Scapegoat, in which all the problems in the company are blamed on a single family member. If only that one person knew how to behave, everything would be all right. The real source of the problem and the responsibility others should take for it are not recognized. Instead, the same black sheep is blamed over and over again for all that is wrong in the organization. Frequently, it is the irresponsible kid brother. But did he ever have a chance?

Finally, there is the Myth of the Messiah, the notion that redemption and salvation will come from an omnipotent outsider. The unfortunate person anointed as the messiah walks into an environment overburdened with expectation: he or she will right every wrong in the organization. Of course, no one can live up to that kind of expectation; the messiah figure is set up to fail. The high turnover of consultants in family firms is symptomatic of this process in action.

Given all the difficulties involved in working in family firms, it is only reasonable to ask if there are any advantages to be found in joining one. The answer is yes. Let us turn now to several.

One important psychological factor—one that is not usually made explicit—is that family firms offer their owners an illusion of immortality. To have one's name on a building or on a product generation after generation gives a sense of continuity. After all, one of the most difficult things for most of us to accept is the temporary nature of our existence.

To turn to more pragmatic reasons, for many people the most attractive aspect of being part of a family firm is the ability to control one's own destiny. In addition, the financial rewards, both immediate and anticipated, are usually great. From a broader socioeconomic perspective, much can be made of the fact that family firms characteristically make longer-term commitments (to both employees and customers) than other firms. A family name, whether attached to a product or a service, stands for something; it is maintained by a sense of tradition and pride. In this respect, family firms can be very different from publicly held companies. Too many of the latter are slaves of the stock market, driven by short-term results. A family firm is also safer from takeover bids. There is no need to look constantly over one's shoulder for the shadow of a corporate raider.

Many family firms are run in a less bureaucratic, less impersonal way than public companies. It is often much easier to get access to senior management. Operations can be more flexible. Decisions can be made more quickly. Since it is often the top executives' own money that is at stake, management does not have to go through elaborate safety checks to arrive at a decision. Furthermore, employees are more likely to feel like part of the family, making for group cohesion and a greater sense of belonging. Not surprisingly, many family firms have a very strong corporate culture.

Another advantage in some family firms is that younger members get an early opportunity to show their mettle (an advantage that works against those people whose early efforts brand them as unsuccessful). This early advancement often makes good sense, since those given heavy responsibilities have heard the family business discussed at breakfast and at the dinner table from the time they were very young. Family firms, with this tendency to place young people in very responsible positions, contrast sharply with large, publicly held corporations; in the latter, you are likely to be quite gray-haired, or have no hair at all, before they let you loose. By that time you may no longer have much fire left in your belly!

So is the family firm still for you? If the answer is yes—if you are not disturbed by its negative aspects and are willing to take a chance—let me give you some pragmatic advice on how to go about starting and maintaining such a firm. Given the high casualty rate of family firms, you will need some survival guidelines. What steps can you take to prevent disaster?

1.   A good first step is to set up some kind of family council whose major task is precisely defining the aims and procedures for the company. What is the firm trying to accomplish? Is it a long-term business, or does the family envision going public and selling out? And if the latter is the objective, what would be an equitable distribution of the proceeds? What financial settlements will be made if a family member wants to leave the business? Arriving at a consensus regarding the overall family vision, along with some of these particulars, helps to develop trust—an all-too-scarce commodity among family members.

2.   If the family intends to stay in business long-term, it is sensible to "professionalize" management and try to follow some of the practices found in public companies; a seat-of-the-pants operation will go only so far. The role of strategic planning, for example, must be emphasized in order to avoid the *Alice in Wonderland* syndrome: "If you don't know where you're going, you may end up somewhere else." In addition, there should be carefully designed incentive systems for non–family members. Moreover, non–family members must have the possibility of reaching top management positions; otherwise, the best and the brightest will not stay around. On the other hand, it is important that family members have some business experience

outside the company. Achieving something outside the family business encourages self-esteem and confidence. Family members who never leave the fold may always be haunted by the question of whether they could have done it on their own—and this perception may be shared by others in the company. To arrive at some form of individuation is important to all of us.

3.　It does not hurt to have a board of directors with real power. Although a rubber-stamp board may seem easier to work with, yes-men and -women are not going to help the company very much. The notion of the usefulness of countervailing power is not a monopoly of public enterprise. It is much better to have a few devil's advocates on the board than to find yourself sitting in an echo chamber. Of course, a proper mandate is necessary to make such a board really effective.

4.　Professional advisers can play an important role in family firms. They can be useful in pointing out the blind spots that can develop in any closed community—a problem to which family businesses are doubly vulnerable, as members are too close to both firm and family to be able to see clearly at all times. Useful professional advisers are accountants, investment bankers, lawyers, tax advisers, and general business consultants. Unfortunately, members of family firms are far more inclined than executives of publicly held corporations to kill the messenger who brings bad news. Studies have shown that only 10 percent of consulting projects for family firms are actually carried through to completion.

5.　Last but certainly not least, there is the question of succession planning—a topic that deserves a book in its own right. Serious attention should be paid to the development of management potential in the next generation. It is essential that expectations be clarified, not be left hanging. What should be the time span for reaching a certain position? How much authority and responsibility should be given to an individual, and at what stage? What does a family member have to do to prove his or her ability? What is fair compensation for those younger members who are *not* going to be top players in the firm? Obviously, if the firm is to survive for many generations, nepotism is not a reliable process by which to address these concerns. If the firm wants to keep family members involved, however, some form of meritocratic nepotism has to be practiced (as in companies such as C&A—a Dutch department store chain—and the Swedish publishing consortium Bonnier).

The prominent French novelist André Maurois once wrote these words:

> A friend loves you for your intelligence, a mistress for your charm, but your family's love is unreasoning; you were born into it and are of its flesh and blood. Nevertheless, it can irritate you more than any group of people in the world.

Obviously, one has to take the good with the bad. In many instances, working in a family firm has a much greater emotional impact than working in a publicly held corporation. But if equanimity and a good sense of harmony prevail, working in a family firm can give an enormous amount of satisfaction.

Reaping the Whirlwind
Creativity at Work

*Nothing is more dangerous than an idea when it's the
only one you have.*

Emilé Chartier

Maturity is the capacity to be immature.

Dave Rioch

One of the advantages of family firms is that they often have the
kind of structure and culture that foster energy and creativity;
in fact, they may be driven by the genius of the founding entrepreneur. Creativity is invaluable—and attainable—in any organization, but if it is not managed properly, it can result in chaos.

Managing logical and orderly left-brain-oriented people is a
pleasant experience. The organizational world suits their specifications. They like analyzing anything and everything, and rules and
regulations make them feel secure. They do what is proper and correct; they conform. In contrast, creative right-brain people are a
pain in the neck; their drummer is slightly off the beat. These people, with their more disorderly, unorthodox, unconventional way of
doing things, can be baffling, and their playful, intuitive methods
can wreak havoc in a by-the-book organization. Because their
thought patterns are divergent, relational, and associative, they deal
with problems by circling them in a zigzag, erratic fashion until
lighting upon a solution.

But before you conclude that the successful organization should root out all right-brain-oriented people like bad weeds, consider this: if you want your organization to go places, if you want to succeed in the global corporate Olympics, you need these creative types. Organizational mavericks are often a source of the innovative products or processes that will help you best the competition.

What differentiates these creative people from common mortals? How can you recognize them? How can you acquire and nurture them in your organization?

In this day and age, it is hard to know what creativity really is. We have a tendency to overuse the word. It is tempting to attribute the potential for creativity to just about anyone. In fact, it is considered derogatory to label someone "uncreative." After all, anything—even the acquisition of a creative bent—is feasible in this age of self-help books and seminars. The power of positive thinking is virtually guaranteed to boost creativity, for only a small amount of money down and low monthly payments.

Hucksters of creativity will argue, "You too can become a famous rocket scientist! You want to become a Nobel Prize winner? Just follow these five easy steps. The reason you aren't there yet is because you haven't realized your creative potential. You have it in you. You need only the proper conditions for your genius to be released and expressed. Your right-brain potential is there, just waiting to be actualized!"

Thus speak modern-day snake-oil salespeople. But what does such an attitude toward creativity imply? All too often the definition of creativity veers from the sublime to the ridiculous as people weigh the value of creative basket weaving, creative Monopoly, or even creative sex. The point that is often overlooked, however, is this: If just anybody can join the creativity "club," is it worth the trouble?

There is something to be said about the populist notion of creativity: most individuals possess a certain amount of unrealized potential and could be more productive, given the right circumstances. Skills can be improved, talent developed. Real creativity, however, necessitates special gifts. I feel that creativity is a rare and often fleeting quality—something to refer to with a capital C. Truly creative people experiment constantly and either apply their knowledge in very novel ways or throw out preconceived ideas altogether; in fact, they often shatter established patterns to produce new paradigms. Thus creativity goes beyond innovation and the implementation of good ideas.

I believe that art and music, inventions and discoveries, and new theories of chaos and order require true creativity. The airplane is an example of a truly creative idea, as was the concept of the wheel in its time. The discovery of penicillin is in the same class as a Mahler symphony, to my mind. Indeed, the conceptualizations of creative geniuses such as Copernicus, Newton, Darwin, Freud, and Einstein form some of the basic principles of Occidental culture.

I see creative people as individuals who possess a considerable amount of conceptual fluency, in that they are able to produce highly unusual ideas very quickly. Wherever a problem may lead, they will follow. They are in fact often able to mentally leap ahead to imagine solutions. They have an enormous amount of energy and willpower. They are also very independent in their judgment and nonconformist in their action, have a sense of playfulness, accept their own impulses, and possess a rich—even bizarre—fantasy life.

Let me elaborate on some of the characteristics of creative people. First, I have to emphasize the importance of curiosity. Truly creative people are unusually inquisitive. They are also intuitive. Intuition is just another form of reasoning, albeit one that depends on unusual channels of information. The heightened intuition of creative people makes them very sensitive to the stimuli around them: they notice things that would be unconsciously screened out by others. This is partly explained by the fact that they are able to handle cognitive complexity; they can visualize forests and at the same time recognize the individual trees. They recognize patterns where others would hear cacophony. Moreover, they internalize their myriad impressions and make connections.

There is a visionary element to the behavior of creative people. They are driven by a sort of "magnificent obsession" toward distant goals. They are persistent and compulsive, and they are not afraid to take risks; although their work may seem effortless to an uninformed observer, in fact it is often a long series of advances and setbacks. Truly creative people are also very autonomous, independent people. Conformity and social norms are not for them; feeling no need to fit in, they dare to be different. Furthermore, creative people are characterized by a high tolerance for ambiguity; they do not aim for premature closure. They can tolerate the tension and suspense that come with leaving questions temporarily unresolved. On the other hand, they are prone to anxiety, perhaps because they are not satisfied with what they produce.

So what about the rest of us? Is it possible to be creative to a small degree and make the most of it? Evidence shows that there is some hope. Attempts to stimulate the process of creativity in less gifted mortals can yield positive results—for example, a tendency toward more divergent (associative) thinking, which tends to be much more fluid and flexible, in contrast to analytical (convergent) thinking.

Earlier in this chapter, I poked fun at some of the garden-variety creativity-boosting techniques currently on the market. Frequently, participants in these activities are left feeling that the only divergence that took place was between them and their money. However, there is a certain value to some of the more serious of these techniques. Although they will not produce an Einstein or a Goethe, they may help change perceptions, opening up a world beyond black or white. At the very least, they help people to recognize creativity in others.

Some of the valid techniques for encouraging creativity include the following:

- Brainstorming: generating new ideas by asking a group of people to suspend critical judgment

- Attribute listing: studying all the basic attributes, properties, and specifications of a problem and searching for alternatives or modifications

- Employing synectics: using analogy and fantasy to make the unfamiliar familiar and vice versa

- Adopting lateral thinking: rearranging information into new patterns

To be honest, it is sometimes hard to differentiate precisely between these various techniques. What they seem to have in common, however, is a suspension of premature critical judgment to enable the free flow of associations.

Some people advocate using mind-expanding drugs as a way of stimulating creativity. At times, doing so can lead to interesting results, to be sure. Samuel Taylor Coleridge's report of his opium-induced dream of Kubla Khan is a good case in point, as is Aldous Huxley's description of his experiments with LSD.

In trying to distill the essence of creativity, some researchers have suggested that there is a sequence of steps in the creative process. According to these researchers, evolution from idea to eventual outcome involves a number of distinct phases: the preparation phase (gathering information about the problem), the incubation phase (mulling over unrelated bits of information, getting the unconscious to work on the problem), the illumination phase (realizing a solution: think of Archimedes running through the streets of Syracuse screaming "Eureka!" after figuring out how to weigh the golden crown of the king), and finally the verification phase (testing the findings).[1]

One can describe the process even more succinctly as the three B's of creativity. These B's refer to situations that stimulate the creative flow. First *bed*—either dreaming or that twilight zone when falling asleep or waking up—when the mind is cut loose from preconceptions and really starts to float. Think of the German scientist

Friedrich August Kekule, who, having dreamed about a snake, was able to figure out the composition of the benzene ring when he woke up. And we already know what happened to Archimedes in the *bath*. The last B stands for *bus* (and in fact includes cars)—vehicles being one of the few places where one can either be alone or at least ignore people (unless carrying a car phone or fax, of course). In these three situations, an almost hypnotic ambience is created. It is the kind of setting where bisociative thinking—making connections where none existed before—is most likely to occur.

If we delve further into the creative process by looking at how particular people became Eureka-shriekers or had "Aha!" experiences, it is interesting to note the frequency of "accidents." Discovery often requires an element of serendipity. Creative people see possibility in unusual occurrences, where others might let them slip by. Think of the consequences if Alexander Fleming had paid no attention to what was happening in his petri dishes. No breakthrough in twentieth-century medicine was more driven by chance than the discovery of penicillin. You may recall that the first detected penicillin spore was borne by a random London breeze through an open window into one of Fleming's dishes. Fleming was able to make sense out of the strange mold that resulted. He was ready for discovery in that he had been working almost exclusively on this type of experiment. As the saying goes, if your mind is a hammer, everything you see looks like a nail. Pasteur once said, "Chance favors the prepared mind."

The creative person is a paradox: he or she is a rebel against conformity but at the same time is very attuned to whatever happens in the environment. Creative individuals are extremely sensitive to the changing needs of their art or science. They are very aware of the fact that there is dissatisfaction with the status quo. They are often the first to recognize that there is a need for revision. Not only that, they do something about it. The truly creative person, to use some hyperbole, is like Prometheus, whose name, after all, literally means "wise before the events." It is as if creative people had some form of prophetic power to look into the future.

How is it that some people acquire this capital-C creativity? What singles them out? Is it a question of inheritance, a trait determined by biological law? Or is it more a result of the kind of developmental experiences these people were exposed to? An interesting corollary question in this context is the connection between creativity and madness. Given a creative person's often unorthodox behavior, it is understandable that such associations come to mind. Where do we draw the line between genius and madness?

Without getting too deeply into the nature-nurture controversy, we can safely assume that genetic factors do play a role; we all start with a certain biological endowment. But superimposed on this biological matrix are our developmental experiences. Even among individuals with a similar biological endowment, these early experiences lead to differences. Of interest to us are the factors in a creative person's upbringing that contribute to their genius.

Think back to when you were growing up. You may remember dealing with two worlds as a child: there was the everyday world, with all its demands, and your own intrapsychic world—a world of inner reality, where drives, wishes, and needs ruled. These outer and inner worlds would later become separate and distinguishable; but when you were a child, a third world existed for you: a space of fantasy and illusion, a place where connections were drawn between the two spheres.

Do you remember the way you played and created an imaginary world? It was an illusionary place between reality and fantasy. It was a world occupied by "transitional objects" such as strings, blankets, dolls, and other playthings—familiar objects that helped link the outer and inner realities. To use the words of the psychoanalyst Donald Winnicott, this world is "the intermediate area of experience between the thumb and the teddy bear." The adult capacity to explore and investigate, the development of an inner sense of cohesion and an external sense of reality, has its beginning in this illusionary space.

This transitional space plays a major role in our development in a very basic way: it serves to help us establish a sense of self-esteem.

For most of us, the transitional world is part of the process of resolving the developmental tasks of childhood to arrive at adulthood and maturity with a unique sense of self. For creative people, however, there is a difference. For most of them, the process never reaches closure; they do not entirely give up their transitional world. Consequently, their involvement in the transitional space continues to affect their behavior throughout their lives.

Parents play a substantial role in this "play area" of the mind. They can be encouraging and help the free flow of associations, or they can stifle it by not giving the developing child enough psychic space. If they are not willing to join in the illusionary processes, they may dam up their child's free play of fantasy and illusion. If parents encourage a child's transitional world, it becomes an incubator for creative thought. This is where such processes as symbolization, make-believe, illusion, day dreaming, playfulness, curiosity, imagination, and wonder all begin.

Every human being uses these processes to some extent, but truly creative people are able to reenter this world as adults much more easily than the rest of us. Consequently, they are familiar with the irrational in themselves and are more in touch with their unconscious. And they never really outgrow this capacity for introspection. As adults, they are able to reach into this transitional world to find unorthodox ideas and solutions. In this context, psychoanalysts have written about the notion of "regression in the service of the ego," meaning the ability to move back and forth between these different worlds and to make the most of the interface.

Broadly speaking, a creative person will follow one of two paths: developing either a constructive form of creativity or, in the case of the less fortunate, a reactive form. In both instances, we are dealing with people who are unwilling to give up their transitional space, but clearly there is an important difference between them.

In the case of someone who exhibits constructive creativity, we can imagine a childhood in which play was encouraged. The parents of such a person played language games with him or her and took the child's transitional objects seriously rather than treating them as something that needed to be cleaned or thrown away. Furthermore, the parents took part in the child's games and applauded curiosity and inquisitiveness. They accepted imaginative and irrational communication; in fact, they enjoyed their child's nonsense. They rewarded independent achievement, giving their child credit for accomplishments, and did not ridicule their child's mistakes. Frequently, we find that these parents were also role models, in that they were autonomous and imaginative themselves.

Of course, parents can push a child too hard, overemphasizing creativity to the point that the child feels inadequate. This situation often occurs when parents have grandiose ambitions for their child in an area in which they themselves have felt frustrated. They want their child to succeed in their place. But in general, gentle, supportive encouragement is appropriate.

For people who are reactively creative, however, the situation is quite different. For them, the transitional world is a refuge from the painful reality of the external world. John Milton's words in *Paradise Lost* are descriptive of this situation: "The Mind is its own place, and in itself can make a Heaven of Hell, and a Hell of Heaven." The transitional space becomes a safe haven from the painful experiences these people had to live through while growing up. But the retreat to this "haven" is not a panacea; a psychic equilibrium cannot always be maintained. At times, various psychological symptoms may result. For example, a number of researchers have shown that there is a higher degree of mood disorders among reactively creative people than is the case for the general population.[2]

Interestingly enough, the linkage between mood disorders and creativity may explain some of the characteristics that contribute to extraordinary talent. Among other things, people who suffer from mood disorders have a higher degree of emotional reactivity: that is to say, they are highly sensitive to external and internal stimuli. Moreover, they have a generous capacity for absorption. This may give them superior concentration; they often have an unusual intensity of focus. In addition, their thought patterns are less structured. This quality gives them free-flowing access to their own unconscious and facilitates novel associations.

What is this reactive mode all about? Why is a transitional space so important to some people? What makes their psychological equilibrium so precarious? Typically, we find that reactively creative people are trying to cope with various forms of traumatic experience. Their environment somehow causes them to be chronically anxious. Giving free rein to their creativity is often their only method for coping with their fears.

The catalyst for their creative preoccupation is frequently something that happened early in their life, at a time when they were most susceptible. For example, the death of a caretaker or another child in the family, serious illness, deformity, excessive sibling rivalry, and external events such as war or being uprooted can be extremely traumatic for a child. Later life experiences, often of a similar nature, may preoccupy the creative adult. Outbursts of creativity seem to help this type of person manage free-floating anxiety and depression or overcome a schizoid state. What stands central is their need for reparation, the need to find a creative solution to their internal struggle.

Examples of creative attempts at reparation are not hard to find in the arts. A common manifestation of this struggle is found in reproductions of internalized body image. Painters' self-portraits, for example, are usually a good "projective indicator" of their state of mind. Just look at the paintings of Munch, Schiele, Kahlo, de Chirico, van Gogh, and Goya.

Edvard Munch once said, "Disease and insanity were the black angels at my cradle." He had witnessed the death struggle of his mother when he was young, and it had a devastating effect on him. This experience may explain his brooding and cataclysmic style of painting. Egon Schiele depicted himself in his paintings in castrated, deformed, and mutilated states. A probable explanation is his troubled childhood, which was punctuated by the deaths of his father and four of his siblings, and a difficult relationship with his mother. Frieda Kahlo, bedridden and incapacitated for long periods of her life (due to the aftereffects of an accident and to polio, which she caught at a very young age), focused her work on distorted representations of the body.

Depression and depersonalization were major elements in the personality of Giorgio de Chirico. His self-estrangement can be found reflected in his paintings, where themes of departure, melancholia, strangeness, eerie emptiness, and stillness predominate. His work was probably influenced by his sister's death and his mother's strong rejection. Not much commentary is needed to explain the tragedy of self-fragmentation as reflected in the work of Vincent van Gogh. In this case, emotional deprivation by a mourning mother, for whom he was supposed to fill the emptiness left by the stillborn first Vincent, had a devastating psychological aftereffect. Francisco Goya's illness, experienced later in life, had an equally dramatic impact on his style of painting. You do not have to be an expert to see the difference between his early and later periods. A gruesome reminder of the change in style is reflected in his painting of Cronus eating his own children.

Painters are not the only ones affected by their life history. Many writers and composers try, in their creative productions, to master their internal struggle. Nikolay Gogol was troubled by body image. It was undoubtedly his enormous nose that prompted him to write the story "The Nose." Franz Kafka's story "Metamorphosis" is very indicative of the kind of self-image he had. His description of his own transformation into a disgusting, monstrous insect needs no further analysis. It was certainly not the outcome of empathic parenting. Those who have read Kafka's "Letter to My Father," explaining the kinds of terrors he suffered during childhood, know what I am talking about. In the case of Edgar Allan Poe, we have a father who deserted the family when Edgar was two and a mother who died of tuberculosis when he was three. Similarly, both of Johann Sebastian Bach's parents died when he was only nine years old. What aggravated this dramatic situation was that not many of his seven siblings survived childhood. No wonder we find so often in his music the themes of death and resurrection. Then we have Gustav Mahler and his "Kindertotenlieder" ("Songs on the Deaths of Children"). These were composed for a reason: many of his siblings died when he was growing up, and his own daughter died as a child. And we should not forget Ingmar Bergman, a man struggling with his antagonists from within, as represented by his stiflingly restrictive parents. This struggle led to highly neurotic but also extremely creative behavior. These are only a few examples; I could go on and on.

Creativity, be it reactive or constructive, is not limited to the fine arts, however. The natural and social sciences also come to mind when we talk about creativity. The construction of the first automobile, the discovery of quantum physics, and the design of the Eiffel Tower undeniably involved an element of genius. Business has its share of creative characters as well, but major contributions to the corporate world do not often create the same kind of excitement that more visible creativity does. Creativity in organizational design tends to be of a subtle nature. Does anyone remember the inventor of double bookkeeping? Who was the person who introduced time-and-motion studies? And what about the first designer of the divisionalized organizational structure or the matrix organization? All of these innovations involved creative steps.

There is another catch to creativity in business: while artists and scientists often work in splendid isolation, this is rarely practical in a business setting. After all, organizations are composed of groups. And with groups come group dynamics. The highly touted ideal of team spirit in organizations can create certain problems, particularly for the more creative types. As I mentioned earlier, such people do not easily conform. A kind of Gresham's Law of Creativity might apply: in this case, it is not bad money that drives out good money but conformists who drive out the creative people. As I indicated in the opening sentences of this chapter, in many organizations creative people are seen as troublemakers. As a result, they *do* get into trouble, and they leave.

How can one manage these mavericks and avoid the loss of potentially valuable people? What can organizational leaders do to attract, develop, and keep creative people in the organization? Perhaps it would be a good idea to think in terms of creative *management*.

The challenge to organizational leadership is to translate mavericks' spontaneous and impulsive behavior into constructive organizational action. Just as parents should encourage a child's imaginative play, senior executives should develop conditions that stimulate innovation and unorthodox methods in their organization.

Richard Branson is good example of an extremely creative executive with an equally creative management style. Branson is the charismatic founder of The Virgin Group, an empire now (after the sale of the record business) best known for its highly successful airline and Megastore retail chain. Branson's way of running his empire has become part of popular folklore. He is not only one of the richest people in the world but also an international celebrity. In the United Kingdom, Branson has reached folk-hero status, and he has been hailed in surveys there as a role model not only for teenagers but also their parents. He has been nominated for awards for enterprise and been voted the most popular businessman of the year.

As an organizational designer, Branson is highly unusual. He has no real corporate headquarters (it used to be a houseboat on the Thames), something you would not expect from someone who employs 6,000 people in more than fifteen countries. Status and the perks of power are not for him. To Branson, decentralization is a religion. He strongly believes that when there are more than seventy people in a building, they should be split into new entities or they risk losing their identity. The company's operating style is characterized by informality, casual dress, a lack of hierarchy, a comfortable environment, and an absence of conformity. As a matter of fact, Branson makes it a point to attract mavericks to his company—and he enjoys the maverick role very much himself, as his madder exploits, such as his balloon and speedboat adventures, illustrate.

At The Virgin Group, lateral communication is the norm. Branson likes the idea of the boundaryless organization. He encourages people to move around; he does not want them to be stuck in narrowly defined jobs. He believes in organic growth, not in raiding other businesses to get market share. Furthermore, he feels that when someone has a creative idea, that person should always have access to resources. In that respect, he serves as a super project champion, nurturing others to develop ideas and bring them to fruition. He believes in the concept that it is better to ask forgiveness than to ask permission. He likes people to take risks, but he also likes to manage the risks. And the reward systems for people who navigate the shoals of risk well are designed accordingly: individuals who have creative ideas for new businesses get a piece of the action. It is Branson's way of holding on to his executives; he wants them to become millionaires under the Virgin umbrella.

Basically, he is trying to create in his company a community of people who collaborate and help each other and at the same time experience fun and excitement. Having fun is a central value of Virgin's corporate culture. And as a well-known prankster, Branson often sets the example. In emphasizing the importance of fun, he is following the simple school of thought that happy people are productive people. Moreover, whatever Virgin is involved in, he wants the company to be the best, not necessarily the biggest. By setting high performance expectations, he encourages his people to rise to the challenge. His airline, Virgin Atlantic, is a good example of this philosophy.

So what can we learn from the Virgin case as far as creative management is concerned? It demonstrates that to manage creatively, a number of organizational, cultural, and leadership steps have be taken. Let us look first at the *organizational* variables that make for a creative workplace.

It may be worthwhile to take a hard look at the structure of your organization. Is it predominantly bureaucratic or organic? Obviously, a fluid, flexible, boundaryless structure is to be recommended. A highly formalized environment tends to have a stifling effect on creativity. Decentralizing the organization also helps, since decentralization tends to be linked with accountability, responsibility, and having a direct feedback link; as a result, it contributes to employees' feelings of control. Having a sense of control over one's environment, as stress research has indicated, creates a buffer against stress and makes one feel better, which in turn has a positive effect on work.

There tends to be little room for creativity in strictly hierarchical organizations—those that have many layers of management. To get the best out of creative people, a high degree of freedom is key. These people, more than others, need to feel that they are in charge of their work and ideas. Excessive reporting and standardized procedures therefore prove to be counterproductive.

On the other hand, the company should have performance evaluation and compensation systems that reward innovation. Is there an appropriate reward system through which the creative people behind a successful project are singled out for recognition? Do they share in the perks and bonuses in appreciation for their contribution? Although potential rewards are not the main motivator for creative people—it is much more important to them to see their ideas realized—giving these successful contributors a piece of the action can do wonders for their sense of equity.

There should also be frequent and easy lateral communication in the organization, in order to stimulate learning and new ideas. *Bypassing* should not be a dirty word. People who work in the organization should not be forced to go through specific channels, and jobs should not be narrowly defined. Task interdependency and job rotation can also be useful, because knowing the details of other jobs leads to a broader point of view. The existence of multidisciplinary teams is also a plus.

Human resource management is another critical area. Efforts should be made to accept diversity. There should be an openness to nonconformists in the organization, because their ideas make for intellectual ferment. They are most likely the ones who ask the unusual questions. They may also be the ones who come up with more effective ways of organizing, and they may identify new product niches. There should be a place for them.

There are some other organizational issues worth considering. For example, what are the physical facilities like? Is the work done in the kind of environment that stimulates the creative juices, or is the workplace such that it reminds you of one of the Stalinist structures so often encountered in Eastern Europe?

Last but certainly not least among the organizational variables, it is very important that the company has the necessary resources—financial, material, and human. Are facilities or funds available for work that initially appears unprofitable or unrelated to the company's vision? Are these resources relatively easy to come by? A person who must continually fight for resources and time to commit to a project is being mentally boxed in and is unlikely to produce much.

The *corporate culture* introduces another set of variables. What are the value and belief systems like? Does a risk-taking ethos exist in the company? Can people make mistakes? Remember, if people are not allowed to make mistakes, they will not make any decisions or take any risks. Creative people do not last long in this sort of situation.

Access to information is another important factor. A company culture that generates secrecy may be good for building paranoia but does not make for a cooperative and collaborative atmosphere. It does not allow the kind of ambience that encourages people to help each other. On the contrary, it is more likely to lead to turf wars.

Actually, many of these dimensions can be summarized in the word *trust*. If there is no sense of trust in the organization, if people are preoccupied with protecting their backs, the psychological contract between individual and organization will break down, and creativity will be one of the first casualties.

In considering all these suggestions, we should not forget about the fun factor (remember Virgin). Normally, having fun rarely comes to mind when we think about organizations, yet a light-hearted attitude toward work helps avoid a buildup of stress and tension. And in the long run, people who have fun are more creative and usually work harder.

Finally, I should mention that a key value of corporate culture is openness to change. Executives have to create a protean organization—one that has the capacity to learn and change. Where there is no change, there can be no creativity.

The third variable that can stimulate creativity in organizations is the *role of leaders*. What is the leadership style like in an organization? Is it democratic and participative, or is it rather autocratic? Naturally, creative people feel much more at ease with the former. In fact, autocratic leadership kills creativity, because people in an autocratic organization do not question the way things are done; they simply conform. It is important that people have the feeling that they can disagree.

What about shared vision? Do people have a good idea of what the organization is trying to accomplish? Are goals clear enough? While these goals need not be very detailed, some form of general direction is needed, and it can often be provided by role models, mentors, or idea champions. An organization needs such people— whatever name they may be given—to set an example.

Training and dedication play important roles in the generation of new ideas. A creative outcome may look accidental, but usually it is the result of a lot of preparation and hard work. Of course, there is an element of luck involved; but as I have discovered personally, the harder you work, the luckier you get. Not only must people be well prepared; they must also be willing to try and try again, in spite of setbacks.

Creative people should be challenged and made to feel essential to the organization. Top managers must empower their people by expressing their expectation that people will do creative work. And leaders should be prepared to nurture the crazy ideas people come up with. If you set high expectations and provide the necessary resources, people try to oblige.

Creativity in organizations is a very delicate flower. Not much is needed to kill it. If you are not careful, the creative people will leave (or not be attracted to the organization in the first place). In this regard, the attitude of the organizational leadership is critical. Leaders should be quite aware of the attitude they disseminate in their organization. They should not forget that they are the ones who set the tone. For example, a belief system that says that there is only one way of doing things, that there is only one right answer to a problem, by definition precludes creativity. Leaders who cultivate the "not-invented-here" syndrome can have a very negative effect. A related problem is a kind of parochialism in which people say that something is not their area. In organizations troubled by these problems, venturing into uncharted territory is seen as too risky. These attitudes should be interpreted as danger signs.

And finally, some leaders I have met feel that play is frivolous; they believe that one should not be foolish. I advise them to keep in mind the creative person's need for a transitional space. If that space is blocked, how can one really be creative? To stimulate creativity, organizational leaders must be willing to accept underdeveloped ideas and bend the rules. They should tolerate ambiguity and show empathy. In addition, they should be willing to make quick decisions rather than always proposing elaborate committees to study ideas. Last but certainly not least, as I have said before, they should allow mistakes (and not dwell on them). Remember, chaos breeds life, while order breeds habit. Whereas your habits are very easy for your competition to copy, creative talent in your organization is a unique asset.

CEOs Also Have the Blues

Succession and Retirement

It is not that I'm afraid to die. I just don't want to be there when it happens.

Woody Allen

Growing old is like being increasingly penalized for a crime you haven't committed.

Anthony Powell

I have measured out my life with coffee spoons.

T. S. Eliot

In a number of the preceding essays, I looked at situations that most CEOs run across at some point in their career. To bring closure to this theme of the career life cycle, I want to address in this essay an issue that all leaders face and that many of them have a great deal of difficulty addressing: the end of their career—a passage that often raises painful questions about self-worth and mortality.

A concern that regularly comes up in my seminars for top executives goes something like this: "I'm fifty-five years old. I've now been the president of this company for more than five years. The idea that I'll continue to do the same thing for another ten years frightens me silly. What do you recommend I should do?" There are no easy answers to this conundrum. Of course, it is tempting to say, "Well, quit." But quit to do what? To go where? It is very difficult for many people to know what to do for an encore after having been a CEO, particularly if they have worked for a big corporation. The power, the perks, the mystique that go with the job can be really addictive. After having had such a heady experience, almost any other job is bound to be a letdown.

The sense of malaise that such people experience after having been in the job too long is nothing to laugh at. It touches the core of their being, shaking their self-esteem. It is anything but easy to come up with a quick response to the question of what they can do with the rest of their life and how they can make that activity a meaningful experience.

Apart from the personal agenda of such people (by which I mean how the job—and a departure from it—affects their mental health), other factors need to be given some consideration. We all know that CEOs have an enormous effect on the lives of the other persons in the organization. It is this that makes the question of how to ensure that CEOs function in a healthy, creative, effective way such an essential one. What can be done to minimize the dysfunctional effects that may result if CEOs overstay their welcome? Unfortunately, the Spanish saying that fish start to stink at the head contains a lot of truth!

Maybe you recognize the CEO blues yourself. Maybe you are beginning to experience similar feelings of disquiet and unease. Maybe you have the sense that the longer you do the job, the more it feels like more of the same. The routine is getting to you. Perhaps you are looking for new thrills; perhaps the time has come to call a spade a spade and admit (difficult as it may be) that you are getting bored with what you are doing. If that is the case, would it not be better to do something about the situation rather than let things slide?

I have often wondered what is the optimum length of time for a CEO to be in a job. What is the point at which enthusiasm, motivation, and commitment start to decline? How much time has to elapse before the CEO becomes less effective? When is the right time to do something else?

It is not easy to find agreement on these points among CEOs. Responses tend to vary widely. After all, the answers depend on a great many variables. For example, are you operating in a highly turbulent or a relatively stable environment? What kind of pressures are you under from the different stakeholders (the board of directors, institutional shareholders, the stock market, banks, customers, venture capitalists)? Do you work for a family-controlled firm? (This factor can make a big difference: the owner of a company may have quite another outlook on commitment and motivation than the head of a public corporation.)

The responses I usually hear from CEOs about the optimum time for doing what they are doing is ten years, plus or minus two. Some studies have shown, however, that around 50 percent of CEOs are likely to remain more than twelve years on the job.[1] This latter figure may be skewed by family-controlled and entrepreneurial firms, of course; in some instances, a family member or entrepreneur may become a CEO at a fairly young age, and he or she may stay in the position for an extremely long time. Think of people such as Armand Hammer of Occidental Petroleum and William Paley of CBS. These people had to be carried out of their respective organizations in a coffin. A time limit was not part of their career planning. Personally, I tend to favor the magical number eight. In my opinion, eight years is probably the period of maximum effectiveness for most people in what can be a very stressful job.

Usually, people who become CEO do so when they are in their early fifties. Many *potentially* productive years lie ahead. The question is this: How many of these years are going to be *truly* productive? How long can a CEO be an effective leader? Envisioning, energizing, empowering, structuring, controlling, and rewarding—the roles of a leader—can be very draining processes indeed. How long can a CEO go on motivating the troops? How long can that person make the organization dance, stimulating creativity, innovation, and productivity?

Is there such a thing as a life cycle for CEOs? Do people in this top position follow a certain pattern? And if so, does a sequence of stages exist? How does it all unfold?

Just as there is a product life cycle—a period during which a product secures sales and profits—there is a life cycle governing the returns produced by a CEO. (It is perhaps useful to bear in mind that product and technology life cycles have become shorter and shorter, putting enormous pressure on CEOs to keep up with events.) Looking at the performance of the CEO on the job, we may be able to distinguish this second kind of life cycle.

Conceptually, it could be said that CEOs pass through three stages on the job, starting with the entry stage, during which experimentation may take place, continuing with the consolidation stage, and ending with the decline stage. (In some cases, however, the latter stage may be recognized and avoided, leading to a period of renewal.) In previous chapters, I have discussed the first two stages; here I will concentrate on the third.

Let us suppose that things have worked out well for the CEO during the first two stages of leadership. Having built up credit with the various constituencies and consolidated a power base, this executive is increasingly in a position to actualize his or her dreams, the preoccupations derived from the inner theater. As time goes by, the CEO may begin to focus more and more on one particular theme, a pattern that may reflect a deep-seated wish or a thread running through that person's life. A particular preoccupation may dominate to the point that it becomes a holding pattern from which it is increasingly difficult to deviate.

Thus as life comes increasingly under control, the CEO settles into a routine. What stands out at this particular juncture is the repetitiveness of a particular theme; the CEO is striving for mastery of an issue that has never really been completely resolved—something that he or she is still struggling with, consciously or unconsciously. What is worrisome, however, is that any deviation from this theme may no longer be welcome; rigidity begins to set in.

Consequently, substantially new initiatives can no longer be expected. From the CEO's point of view, the excitement of mastering new things is disappearing. The only changes made are incremental ones. The only thing that counts is the fine-tuning of this major theme, which has been an essential part of the CEO's preoccupations, a pillar of his or her self-concept. Subordinates who undertake to question the theme or strategy do not do so lightly; on the contrary, they know that they do so at their own peril.

What are the indications that a CEO has reached this particular phase in the career cycle? One major indication is that there is not much change in the product portfolio: no new products are foreseen for the near future. In addition, the composition of the existing customer base may seem static, and no initiatives are in hand to recruit new ones. Furthermore, there is no new blood brought into the organization. The company sticks to the same tired old group of senior executives—those who are committed to the particular orientation of the CEO. And the company is accumulating too much cash. Top executives are running out of ideas about how to use the available money.

It is during this third phase that the problems start, both for the organization and for the CEO. What is happening to the CEOs at this stage? They seem to be stuck; myopia sets in; they stop listening. Points of view at odds with their own are no longer welcomed. They are likely to come down heavily on opposition. Moreover, the job itself no longer gives them enough stimulation; the routine gets to them. Becoming bored with what they are doing, they may start to coast. They may begin to sound like a needle stuck on a record, harping on that one theme that has now become overfamiliar to all. Because the old excitement is gone, performance may begin slacking off.

For a good example of such behavior, we can look at Sewell Lee Avery, who once was the chairman of Montgomery Ward, a large U.S. department store chain. Avery was preoccupied with cost cutting and liquidity (he feared an imminent depression), a theme that had proved to be quite effective when he was holding other positions. Unfortunately, at Montgomery Ward his obsession led him to turn the company into a bank with a department store front. His particular preoccupation left customers with very little to buy—a state of affairs that did nothing to further the interests of the company.

Ken Olsen, the founder and former chairman of Digital Equipment Corp., is another case in point. Olsen can be considered one of the pioneers of the computer business. His vision of the computer industry was once exactly in tune with the needs of the consumers. However, his continued preoccupation with technical perfectionism and his failure to pay much attention to changing consumer needs led to organizational rigidity and poor adaptation to the market. This hurt profits tremendously, caused a dramatic fall in the price of shares, and led to his forced retirement.

For various reasons (the origin of which lies in the inner theater), these CEOs found it very hard to adjust to changes in the external environment. Their stubbornness in clinging to one particular theme even when its time was past eventually became dysfunctional and led to their downfall. Naturally, such a decline is more rapidly noticeable in industries characterized by a highly dynamic, turbulent environment. Executives who operate in a relatively stable environment can carry on in the same routine for a longer period, since less innovation is required of them.

This third phase can have a devastating effect on the company. Leadership's holding on to a theme that has become outmoded or redundant can be disastrous. In some cases, it may even bring the company to bankruptcy.

Many variations on this scenario are possible. Some CEOs may start to distance themselves from day-to-day company activities, becoming increasingly remote. Needing new mental stimuli, they may become interested in other things—issues related to the organization only peripherally if at all—while at the same time maintaining their old routines. They may spend more time outside the office pursuing different, more glamorous interests, such as social or sporting events.

All this would be perfectly acceptable in a CEO capable of delegating and letting go. Unfortunately, lessened involvement with the details of the business does not always go hand in hand with increased delegation. The CEO may secretly fear that delegation might encourage subordinates to question the theme he or she is pursuing (and to discover that it is no longer appropriate).

Some CEOs may squander scarce company resources on excessive perks, such as company airplanes, company retreats, or special company events. Others may get involved in risky new ventures. They may see the merger and acquisition route as a solution to their sense of inner unrest—a way of getting kicks, however costly they may turn out to be. Consequently, they may embark on rather ineffective efforts at empire building at the company's expense. Still others may become involved (quite commendably) in social concerns, such as sponsorship of the arts. This social involvement is quite all right, as long as it does not come at the cost of running the business.

Lee Iacocca's well-publicized and time-consuming external activities—fund-raising for the Statue of Liberty and toying with the idea of becoming a candidate for president of the United States at a time when Chrysler was still struggling to keep afloat—are examples of good ideas that were badly timed. As president of SAS, Jan Carlzon's preoccupation with acquisitions and the media is another case in point. In both examples, questions arose regarding who was running the company, taking care of day-to-day business. These kinds of developments, combined with an unwillingness to change a previously successful theme, are symptoms of a period of decline.

This decline may be accelerated if the board fails to execute its review functions properly. Once a CEO has proven his or her mettle, the board may allow increasing latitude. This is especially likely if the CEO has filled the board with people who, because they are indebted to the top executive, know not to take their review function too seriously. It does not help that in many instances board members overidentify with the problems of the CEO. (After all, many of them were CEOs themselves.) Furthermore, it is not easy to ask people to whom one feels close to change their act or get out. Thus many company boards have a tendency to turn a blind eye, taking action only when things become really catastrophic—by which time it is often too late.

Less directly connected with work, but often related to it, is another, more personal set of considerations that may contribute to a CEO's decline. Perhaps a good way to illustrate what I mean is to tell you about a dream once recounted to me by an executive who had passed the midlife point, someone who had become increasingly anxious about the challenges ahead. This man described a dream he had had in which he was sitting in front of his computer trying to finish a report. Things seemed to be going well until suddenly a sense of panic washed over him. He had a foreboding that something terrible was going to happen. When he looked once more at the computer screen, the text he had been working on was no longer readable but was dripping down. Everything he had written was scrambled; all the work he had done was incomprehensible and useless. The dream took a terrifying turn as the screen changed into a kind of mirror in which he could see his own face, horribly distorted. He woke up sweating and very frightened.

Talking about his dream, this executive referred to his growing feeling that his work was meaningless. He sensed that his job was not really leading anywhere. What was the use of surpassing the annual plan one more time? Of beating the budget? Of increasing market share? He also worried whether he would be able to keep up the kind of pace required. In short, what he was really concerned with, as the imagery of the dream implied, was the possibility that he might fall apart. His panic was exacerbated by the chest pains from which he had recently been suffering. He wondered if he had a serious disease.

Compare the dream of this executive with the troubled opening lines of the *Divine Comedy*, which Dante wrote at a time when he was going through a considerable midlife crisis. He had been banished from his native city of Florence and was wondering about his identity and career:

> Midway in our life's journey, I went astray
> from the straight road and woke to find myself
> alone in a dark wood. How shall I say
> what wood that was! I never saw so drear,
> so rank, so arduous a wilderness!
> Its very memory gives a shape to fear.

The dream of the executive and the opening lines of Dante's poem give us some insights into the kind of issues important to people as they approach middle age. To start with (and probably most important), midlife brings a greater awareness of aging, illness, and the dependency that may come with them. As the executive's dream indicates, growing older is accompanied by many transformations. We may have appreciated these facts at one level when we were younger, but our degree of understanding was different then from what it is now. These were issues of an abstract nature in our earlier years; they did not really hit home then and could not be taken personally. For the young, death is just a distant rumor. For those who are under forty, it is easy to believe that these issues do not apply personally—and maybe it is better that way.

After midlife, things become quite different. We begin to see time differently. We have the sense of its becoming finite; we realize that there is only so much of it left. We begin to think in terms of time left to live as opposed to time since birth. The idea of our death can no longer be ignored, particularly as peers or mentors age and die—people who have been important to our inner mental map and whose death causes feelings of disquiet. Before the age of forty, we really believe that we are immortal; after that point, though, it dawns upon most of us that time is limited. We become increasingly aware of the inevitability of death and the fact that it is coming closer.

What really brings that point home is looking in the mirror and seeing how our face is changing. As the executive discovered in his dream, this can be a terrifying experience. As Jean Cocteau once said, the mirror is the place where one can see death.

Cocteau's statement holds a certain amount of truth, because the mirror forces us to acknowledge that certain things *are* happening to our body. We must not forget that the ego is first and foremost a body ego. Bodily image (including the face) plays an important role in stabilizing identity. Physical transformations can have an enormous psychological impact and strongly affect our outlook on life. Physical aging leads to greater body monitoring and an increase in hypochondriacal anxiety.

These changes include the obvious ones, such as losing hair or turning gray, having to wear glasses, developing a paunch or sagging breasts, developing wrinkles or dental problems. Those women who are particularly narcissistically predisposed—women who are inclined to rely largely on their physical appearance for getting attention and managing their sense of self-esteem—find it particularly difficult to deal with the noticeable effects of aging and the changes in their body image. Although they may try to fight the aging process and may even win a few early battles, in the long run they will lose the war. After all, how many face-lifts can you have?

For men, the greatest narcissistic injuries that come with aging have to do with facial changes and sexuality. Many men experience serious fears about their decrease or loss of sexual potency, discovering at midlife that they can no longer hold on to the fantasy of themselves as a kind of Don Juan.

Although CEOs may not talk about such issues in public, friends and co-workers may get a sense of them through locker-room jokes. Of course, where they are really spelled out is in encounters with therapists. Dealing with the loss of sexual potency is very difficult for many individuals. It can be an underlying cause of diffuse feelings of irritation and anger. In addition, it may lead to resentment about the behavior of younger people; it may arouse envy—one of the major equalizing forces in human life—toward the next generation, who seem unfairly free from such worries. As a consequence, some executives may resort to displaced aggression and act out their feelings. This is one of the reasons that I often argue that the mythological King Laius is alive and well and living in organizations. In a symbolic way, "fathers" may want to kill their "sons." I have encountered a number of senior executives who, upset about those things they cannot change (the aging process and their decreasing sexual prowess, in particular), take their frustration out on other, younger executives. In this way, they show the world that they still have power, even if it is of another order.

If you encounter an organization experiencing a high turnover of younger executives—one in which statements such as "We give our younger executives lots of responsibility" turn out to be double-edged, since very few young executives pass their test and are proven worthy—it is very possible that there is a King Laius on the loose. The many dramatic succession stories we read about in the financial pages may be related to similar psychodynamic difficulties. These stories usually concern senior executives who are reluctant to make way for the next generation. Instead, when the younger, rising stars are perceived as becoming too powerful, they are forced out.

The decrease in potency and the existence of generational envy are related to the very reasonable worry of some CEOs about whether they continue to be effective in the workplace. CEOs in this stage may experience an increasing sense of entrapment and a fear of obsolescence. They may begin to feel imprisoned by routine, aware that they are no longer learning, that they are decreasingly productive.

One way in which some of these executives express their negative feelings is to say that they feel bored. However, as any psychologist will tell you, boredom is a complex state of mind that can be a cover-up for many negative emotional feelings, including free-floating anxiety, restlessness, irritability, nervousness, and depression. Whatever the cause, such feelings are not at all conducive to job satisfaction and productivity.

Some CEOs have a different problem. As a direct result of their past success in the job, they start to feel fraudulent, like an impostor. Despite their evident and tangible achievements, they begin to wonder whether they really are as good as other people think they are. They attribute whatever success they have to luck, compensatory hard work, or superficial factors such as physical attractiveness or likability. People troubled by these irrational thought processes find it hard to accept their own talents and achievements. They have somehow absorbed the notion that they have fooled everyone around them. Although this attitude may not have been problematic when they started on the career ladder, with success comes the increasing dread that they will finally be found out. They are preoccupied by an irrational concern that people will discover their feet of clay. Such preoccupations predictably cause a considerable amount of anxiety.

Lingering in the minds of people who feel like impostors are perfectionistic attitudes about themselves. These feelings originated in the way these people were treated while growing up. In all likelihood, the family dealt with the achievements of these developing children in the wrong way, causing confusion in their mind about the extent to which achievements were the result of their own efforts. As such children grew up, they began to distrust their parents' perceptions (and consequently their own). Their achievements and capabilities were experienced as phony and hollow. No wonder that such children view themselves as frauds; no wonder that they cannot enjoy their achievements even as adults.

The matter may be further complicated by an unconscious sense of anxiety about doing better than their parents. This anxiety may be accompanied by an equally unconscious fear that the parents may become envious and retaliatory. In these cases, the Oedipal stage seems likely never to have been satisfactorily resolved. Because proper identification with the parents has never taken place, parental relationships remain fraught with conflict.

Infantile fears about retaliatory envy, which may well contain a kernel of truth inferred from covert messages, may linger on into adulthood. These feelings may be exacerbated by the tendency for success to elevate the individual from the family background, raising realistic fears of separation, estrangement, and rejection. Thus moving up the career ladder brings not pleasure but rather an intensifying amount of trepidation and anxiety.

Many executives, having reached a top position, begin to ask themselves, "What next? Is that all there is to life?" For some, finally reaching the position they have been striving for all their life can come as a real letdown. Instead of bringing pleasure to these people, the achievement creates a deep sense of disappointment. These executives may suffer from what can be called the Faust syndrome—the melancholia of having everything completed. What they saw as their life's task has been achieved; there is nothing to strive for any longer. Those who are unable to look for new challenges may become quite depressed.

Other nonwork issues preoccupy these executives. Many begin to worry increasingly about their relationships with their children and their spouse. They realize that the balance of their attention has been very lopsided, directed mainly toward their work. They feel that they are losing contact with their children and often have a hard time dealing with their children's increasing independence. They do not always like what they see or how their children are turning out. Consequently, some of them make a desperate effort to change the kind of behavior in their children that they find unacceptable. But at this late stage, there is not much they can do about it. The time to act was earlier—when they were unavailable to the family because they were too busy working on their career.

If they had been asked about their relationships when they were younger, most of these people would have revealed a rather instrumental approach to their career, reasoning along these lines: "I'm going to put a lot of effort into my career to start with so that my wife and children will have a better life later on." It is as if they are willing to forgo the present for the sake of the future. Only the future seems to count.

Executives (they are usually men) believe and behave in this way with a vengeance. Most of them spend much more time and energy on their career than they do on their private life. When questioned, they readily express concern about the quality of their private life and claim that they make a conscious effort to put time into it. But when their behavior is analyzed more closely, many of their professed resolutions are revealed as merely wishful thinking. The sad outcome of acting in this manner is that their spouse and children are no longer around when they have finally accomplished what they set out to do. In postponing gratification in this way, they miss intimate family moments—moments that will never return. At midlife, when the chickens have come home to roost (and far too late in the day), they want to make up for lost time. Their concern about the here and now should have started much earlier. Making changes in their family relationships and the behavior of their children at this late stage is not going to be easy.

Tensions in the marital relationship frequently form part of this crisis. If the children have already left home, as is often the case, the family is very different. Both partners may worry what life will be like with only the two of them. Will they be able to manage without using the children as an excuse for not dealing with each other? Many couples have great difficulties in handling such a situation. Not infrequently, and not necessarily consciously, they create "problem children" in order to have something to talk about. Likewise, these problem children may delay their departure, staying at home longer. Some couples will do anything to avoid dealing with issues that are of real concern to each other.

Others may start new relationships, have affairs, and eventually divorce. Quite a few people choose this way of revitalizing themselves. Some men start affairs with younger women as a way of denying that they are aging. These are the Peter Pans who want to remain eternally young. Some may even start a new family, hoping that this time they will get things right. They are looking for a second chance.

Some CEOs also find it hard to deal with their spouse's enthusiasm for outside activities. Many women married to a high-flying, often-absent executive have little choice but to stop working when their children are born in order to spend time with them. Once the children become more independent, these women may start picking up the threads of their previous career. Their renewed energy and outside interests can arouse the resentment and envy of their husband, particularly if he is tired and bored with his own job.

An additional source of stress for individuals at this midlife point is the undeniable evidence that their parents are aging. Witnessing the mental and physical decline of one's parents can be extremely disturbing. Some people may interpret parental decline as a harbinger of their own fate, an indication of what might be in store for them, a caricature of what they dread happening to themselves; they see their parents' impending death as a reminder of their own mortality. The increasing dependence of their parents also necessitates their assuming a new and different role. This reversal of traditional roles of authority and submission vis-à-vis their parents is distressing and hard to adjust to.

I have met a number of executives who suffer from what has been described as "anniversary reaction." By this I mean an initially undefined form of anxiety that upon closer analysis appears to be related to the anniversary of the death of a loved one. It is most commonly experienced as a state of depression and is basically a strong emotional reaction to an earlier event occurring on the occasion of an annual celebration or remembrance. Some executives become especially anxious as they approach the age at which a parent died. As the date gets nearer, a severe crisis can sometimes be precipitated. Some individuals may even experience symptoms similar to those of a deceased (usually same-sex) parent or other person important in their life. Deeply buried conflicts about rivalry and the realization of death wishes may be revived on these occasions. This again makes for complex feelings of unease.

Retirement is similarly and simultaneously becoming a reality that can no longer be ignored, and it is therefore yet another cause for worry. How adequately has it been prepared for? How can it best be dealt with? To those for whom identity is very much bound up in the job, the idea of retirement can be very frightening. While financial concerns undoubtedly play an important part in these worries, the primary source is different: all too often executives fail to plan sufficiently for retirement, both financially and psychologically, simply because they do not want to think about it. That avoidance is understandable, because many for whom work has been everything die soon after retirement.

The question of succession, which becomes unavoidable at this point, is a critical process that is never without conflict. Succession brings many psychological issues to the fore, a major one of which is death anxiety on the part of the person who is to be succeeded. Succession reminds leaders of their mortality, a thought they do not necessarily welcome. Consequently, they may try to circumvent and sabotage the process. They may set traps for their proposed successor, for example. Being made crown prince has proved to be the kiss of death to many individuals. Think only of aspiring leaders working with two executives I have already mentioned: William Paley of CBS and Armand Hammer of Occidental Petroleum. Each ushered out several supposedly certain successors. Those two Titans of business definitely did not go gentle into that good night!

There is an apocryphal story about Konrad Adenauer, the first chancellor of the Federal Republic of Germany, who allegedly once sat his grandson on his knee and asked him about his plans for life. The boy said, "I want to be chancellor like you." Adenauer replied, *"Nein, nein, mein Junge; Bundeskanzler gibt's nur eine."* No, no, young man; there can be only one chancellor. At the time, Adenauer was eighty-seven years old!

Like Shakespeare's King Lear, leaders often seem ready to surrender their authority while simultaneously trying to hold on to their power base. CEOs, who are experts in the economics of power, do not necessarily like it when people start to shift loyalties, when other executives in the company start to pay more attention to the heir apparent. Altogether, letting go can become a very unattractive proposition.

As in Shakespeare's play, generational issues can become extremely unpleasant. The person who has to go may become concerned about his or her legacy, questioning whether the successor will respect what has been built up so painstakingly over the years. And the legacy itself can take many forms, from physical structures, such as an office building or a factory, to the intangibles of corporate culture, such as a specific management philosophy, an idiosyncratic interpretation of the company's mission, or a particular way of doing things in the organization. The urge to protect one's personal legacy may be a powerful block to letting go. It may lead to second thoughts about the wisdom of relinquishing power altogether.

So what advice can we give CEOs who find themselves stuck in the job, equally fearful of losing their effectiveness and of giving up? And how can we create awareness of end-of-career problems in executives who themselves sense no difficulty but are seen by others as losing their hold? The best thing, of course, is for the executives themselves to realize what is happening, acknowledge their increasing ineffectiveness, and look for new horizons while the going is still good. Naturally, a graceful exit would be the preferred choice and is often in everybody's best interest. With hindsight, executives may later see the decision to exit as the wisest one they ever made (painful as it may have been at the time). Going may have given them the jolt they needed to become more effective again, albeit in a different situation.

Executive programs can offer a useful form of stocktaking. The time devoted to reflection and comparison may lead to a feeling of renewal, arresting the CEO's downswing in effectiveness. Such programs offer executives great opportunities to exchange ideas with colleagues who find themselves in similar situations. Going one step further, the CEO may consider the possibility of taking a sabbatical. This option, though appealing, is rarely taken, however, given the reality of organizational politics. Many top executives consider it too risky to be out of circulation for months. They worry (and rightly so) that they may be in for a surprise when they come back; their job may no longer be there. After all, out of sight, out of mind. However, some of the CEOs who have taken the plunge, having set up the company to continue functioning effectively during their absence, have found the sabbatical a very rejuvenating, enriching experience.

Some CEOs choose the generativity route as preparation for their exit, obtaining great pleasure from the role of mentor and from seeing younger executives standing on their own two feet, taking risks and making decisions. Of course, this approach to learning works only if CEOs create a climate of trust and true dialogue within the company, where existing assumptions can be challenged. Taking the generativity route is a way of establishing continuity in the organization. When the next generation is ready, it is to be hoped that such CEOs have the courage to hand over the reins and bow out gracefully.

This generativity option is a truly constructive one. It is a way to create a learning organization and arrest the cycle of birth, growth, maturity, decline, and failure that characterizes far too many companies. CEOs who take the generativity route help organizations develop the capacity to learn from experience and adapt successfully to changes in the environment. Instead of becoming fossilized, such CEOs create a climate where people remain proactive. They help other executives anticipate the demands of the external environment, exploit new opportunities, evolve continuously, and avoid becoming stuck in dysfunctional learning patterns.

The trick here is to create a climate where, because of the nature of the prevailing dialogue, executives continually learn and adapt.

The challenge for many CEOs is to recognize when the moment has come to change course—the moment when, if they do not regenerate themselves, they risk becoming one of the walking dead. If (to continue this morbid metaphor) these executives reach that moment without changing course, they leave a graveyard behind when they eventually leave.

CEOs who decide to look for a new horizon may be pleasantly surprised at the outcome. Some people attempt what I call "doing a Gauguin"—like the artist, they make a complete break from their previous career—and many find the new challenge very fulfilling. When they find the courage to do what they have always wanted to do—perhaps something that they were not allowed or did not dare to do in the past—they finally become their own person; no longer are they acting out a parental or self-imposed fantasy of what they *should* be doing.

Other executives on the brink of retirement find renewed fulfillment in the family, making a concerted effort to get closer to their spouse, children, and particularly newly arrived grandchildren. They try to get in touch with their feelings in an attempt to neutralize the emotionally numbing aspects of their organization. Others find very satisfying roles outside their organization; these can vary from volunteer work for social causes to a greater preoccupation with culture and leisure concerns.

American theologian Reinhold Niebuhr is credited with having said, "God, give us grace to accept with serenity the things that cannot be changed, courage to change the things which should be changed, and the wisdom to distinguish the one from the other." Wise CEOs certainly know what is meant by this.

14

. . . .

Do Workaholics Have More Fun?
Balancing Work and Pleasure

There is more to life than to increase its speed.
                                        Mahatma Gandhi

*What is the use of running when we are not on the
right road?*
                                        German proverb

*I'll bet your father spent the first year of your life
throwing rocks at the stork.*
                                        Irving Brecher

In order to understand behavior patterns—whether they be envi-
able (such as creativity) or destructive (such as the ones we will
examine next, in a look at the darker side of leadership)—it is
important to realize that intrapsychic and interpersonal processes
determine the way we act and make decisions. Over time, through
our interactions with caretakers, teachers, and other influential people, a sort of inner theater develops. The internalized, habitual rules
of conduct that result form the core of an individual's personality
and become the matrix on which behavior and actions are based.
This internal theater influences our behavior throughout our lives.
Leaders are no exception; and unfortunately, a dysfunctional leader
is likely to have a negative effect on his or her organization.

Workaholism is a common type of dysfunctional behavior. Many executives are like human dynamos; they stand out because of their incessant activity. These people get very restless on weekends. They mow the grass twice, wash the car, and clean up the garage, but they still feel itchy. They do not know what to do with themselves when faced with free time. They might not admit it, but in their heart of hearts they really look forward to Monday morning.

Why do they not take some work home? Probably because their family complains that they are never available. Rationally, they too know that they should spend more time with their family. But family time is not really as rewarding as working to these eager beavers. At least at the office, they feel there is some kind of purpose to their life. There are so many things to be done, so many deadlines to meet. At home, their role is far less clear.

Do you recognize yourself from this description? Do you work fourteen to sixteen hours a day? If so, are congratulations in order? People disagree on the answer to that question. Many companies, though, love to have workaholics around. They are both the sergeants and the lieutenants of organizational life. They make things happen. When they are asked to do something, it is sure to be done (although they may grumble, they may complain about overwork, and they may be a pain to work with). But how good they are at working with other people is another issue. Workaholics are usually not very patient. After all, nobody else can do the work as well as they do it (or so they believe); furthermore, nobody is willing to work the kind of hours they do. So workaholics tend to take over from others, wanting to do everything.

Of course, in terms of personal health, they pay a high price for piling up assignment after assignment. Is it really advisable to work seventy to eighty hours a week? "But what the hell," they tell themselves. "At least I get *some* sort of satisfaction out of what I do."

Another way of stereotyping this group of people is to say that they suffer from the Sisyphus complex. Read up on your Greek mythology if you cannot recall the punishment of Sisyphus. He did something nasty to Zeus; and, as you know, Zeus does not forgive easily. He found a choice punishment for Sisyphus: the poor man had to roll a giant rock up a hill. Unfortunately, the task was endless. There was no respite. Whenever, after a lot of effort, Sisyphus managed to push the rock to the top, the rock would roll down again, and he had to start all over.

Workaholics are like Sisyphus. Whatever they do, they feel that their task is not completed; they never feel satisfied. Furthermore, they are their own worst critics. They keep on pushing; they keep on pestering themselves. And they are hard not only on themselves; because workaholics are so driven, those around them often suffer also. It is almost as if they had a little voice in the back of their head telling them that what they have done is not enough, that they can do much better. Oscar Wilde summed up this problem very well when he said, "In this world there are two tragedies. One is not getting what one wants and the other is getting it."

Some people compare workaholics to what has become known in the organizational stress literature as the Type A personality. Type A's could be described as aggressive, inwardly hostile workaholics. It was cardiologists Meyer Friedman and Ray Rosenman who first made the Type A classification in the context of coronary proneness. They discovered—without discounting other factors, such as genetic predisposition, excessive weight, smoking, high blood pressure, lack of exercise, high blood cholesterol, and so on—that certain personality characteristics may contribute to the incidence of heart attacks.

Friedman and Rosenman made a distinction between Type A's and Type B's. While taking into account many of the other contributing factors, their study indicated that Type A's have twice the rate of coronary disease as Type B's. They are also five times more likely to have a secondary coronary attack, and they have twice the rate of fatal heart attacks.

How do you recognize Type A's? It is not all that difficult. Remember the last time you were in a traffic jam? It was the Type

A's who were making all the noise: constantly honking their horns, making rude gestures. Some people describe Type A's as the ideal customers in a restaurant: they eat fast, drink fast, and pay fast. They are really helpful in giving the establishment a high rate of turnover, because they do not hang around after the meal. Someone once said that the ultimate Type A is the person who flushes the toilet before even using it!

Type B's, by contrast, are much more easygoing. They take their time to linger over their food. They enjoy tasting the wine; they are in no hurry to pay the bill and leave.

Basically, Type A's suffer from what we might call hurry sickness. Because they have trouble doing nothing, they are in constant motion. Being very impatient, they try to do two or more things at a time. They tend to hurry or interrupt the speech of other people. They feel constantly compelled to challenge others. They become quite irritable when kept waiting. They are obsessive about being on time; punctuality becomes a matter of pride to them. Type A's also tend to dominate the conversation, often exhibiting explosive speech patterns. Because they feel guilty when relaxing, they try to schedule more and more in less and less time. Workaholics may also have nervous tics and gestures, such as clenching their fists, banging on the table, drawing back the corner of their mouth, laughing in a jarring manner, or grinding their teeth.

Perhaps you were not sure whether or not you are a workaholic when I first presented the question. Do you know now? Have you recognized yourself? Are you one of them?

Some industries and companies can be real shelters for Type A's. In fact, Type A's may be the only people who fit in. Consider, for example, the kind of life investment bankers have on Wall Street; picture what happens inside high-powered advertising agencies. Many consulting firms also tend to attract this kind of personality, as do commodity brokerages.

Researchers analyzing stress have estimated that the number of Type A's in companies fluctuates between 55 and 65 percent.[1] In some go-getting companies, the percentage is even higher. Given the kind of pressure these people experience and their susceptibility to stress, one could speculate that there must be a high rate of personnel turnover in such firms.

With all their running around and their efforts to appear important, do workaholics have more fun? I seriously doubt it. It almost seems as if they are running away from life. As a matter of fact, there is a strong self-defeating component to the behavior of workaholics. They often end up with broken marriages, poor relationships with their children, and a host of psychosomatic symptoms (including, as I mentioned before, heart attacks).

Aldous Huxley, in his book *Point Counter Point*, painted a rather somber picture of these people: "Work gives them the comfortable illusion of existing, even of being important. If they stopped working, they'd realize they simply weren't there at all, most of them. Just holes in the air, that's all."

As far as having fun goes, there is a very hostile component to the behavior of Type A's; in fact, many Type A's are quite angry people. It is their explosive anger and irascibility that are so stressful to them. Because their anger and hostility make for coronary proneness, you could even say that these people are killing themselves. The Japanese have a special term for this: *karoshi*, death from overwork.

Due to the personality makeup of many Type A's, they perceive the world as a very hazardous place. They see danger everywhere. Given the way their perceptual apparatus functions, each encounter tends to activate their fight-flight alarm mechanism. When that sort of pressure is constantly put on the body, it inevitably overloads the system. Resistance wears out, and exhaustion and collapse follow.

As I mentioned earlier, workaholics can be very hard on others. They can be pushy, irritable, and self-righteous. What is worse, they may not even notice that they rub others the wrong way. But workaholics expect nothing of others that they do not expect of themselves.

If we delve a little bit deeper, we find that many workaholics experience a profound sense of insecurity; they seem to have a sense that there is something fundamentally wrong with them. In the essence of their being, some workaholics think that they are unacceptable and unlovable, that others appreciate them only for what they do, not what they are. This makes them very anxious and unsure of themselves. The only positive feelings they have apparently derive from successfully accomplishing particularly challenging tasks. Unfortunately, as I said earlier, the satisfaction they get out of tackling challenges does not last. These people have to deliver over and over again. The old anxiety about not living up to expectations constantly reasserts itself, making this a rather compulsive way of maintaining a precarious sense of self-esteem.

We could interpret the behavior of workaholics as an attempt to please others. These "others," however, seem to be exceptionally demanding and to have extremely high standards. It seems to be almost impossible to satisfy them. And who are these mysterious "others"? As a matter of fact, they are not mysterious at all. The "others" are the people who help us to set standards for ourselves, and the most obvious of these are our parents; they are the most important standard-bearers. After all, they deal with us at a time when we are very impressionable.

Nobel prize winner Elias Canetti once said, "If a mother could be content to be nothing but a mother; but where would you find one who would be satisfied with that part alone?" And as he knew better than many, some parents can be quite demanding. They may burden their offspring with excessive expectations, sending them on a "mission impossible"; in the process, they may forget to take the needs of their children into consideration.

Let me try to explain conceptually what happens when expectations are first set for children by others and then internalized by the children themselves. To do so, I need to borrow two metapsychological concepts from psychoanalytic language: the superego and the ego ideal. (Many psychoanalysts consider the ego ideal to be a set of functions within the superego.) The superego represents a set of prescriptions. It can be looked at as a self-critical agency containing the system of moral codes that is also known as the conscience. It becomes, as it were, the representative of society within the psyche. Behavior that conflicts with the conscience produces guilt.

The ego ideal, on the other hand, sums up a person's classification of goals, ideals, and other values. It stands for the conception of who the individual wishes to be. It is a kind of checklist against which we can compare ourselves. The ego ideal is shaped in the early stages of the life cycle and then modified through growth and experience.

The original sources of superego (and ego ideal) development are the parents and other principal caretakers. While growing up, the child internalizes the prohibitions and restraints of the parents because of a fear of punishment and a need for parental love and approval. Thus parental demands and punitive standards find a resting place in the child's psyche. Later on, of course, siblings, other family members, and teachers all have their own influence. The way in which this process of internalization works determines our individual standards of right and wrong (our conscience) as well as our aims and aspirations (our ego ideal). Thus this agency of the mind, the superego, rewards us with feelings of positive self-esteem when we are "good" (meaning when we live up to these standards) and punishes us when we are "bad." When the latter happens, we experience feelings of shame, guilt, and low self-esteem.

Unfortunately, not all parents introduce these standards gently. Some of them, if they have not succeeded in their own aspirations, may want a second chance. They want their children to succeed for them. Many parents who live vicariously through their children put excessive demands on them. In the process, the children's own wishes and desires may be ignored; the children cannot be themselves. Because they are dependent on their parents, they have no choice but to put up a false front and give in. After all, the adults are so much more powerful than they are. When children are sent on this sort of "mission impossible," it is generally because the parents have been instrumental in burdening them with an excessively severe superego.

What makes this phenomenon even more intractable is that much of what goes on in the internalization of standards happens beyond conscious awareness. Instead, workaholics consciously experience (though without knowing the source of the sensations) free-floating anxiety, restlessness, feelings of insecurity, and problems of self-esteem.

Not surprisingly, Type A parents create Type A children. Laboratory studies centered around the interaction between parents and children have shown that parents of high Type A's criticize and praise their children more, tend to compare their achievements with those of other children, and give their children more instructions about how required tasks are to be done. This parental pressure promotes a constant need for high achievement, fear of failure, and the inclination to overreact in competitive situations. According to one study, the children of Type A parents end up being a lot more anxious, insecure, and prone to stress symptoms than their peers.[2]

The major preoccupation of workaholics, then, is to cater to the harsh standards that they have internalized. For quite a few of them, the process of trying to please the parents of childhood never stops. Whatever efforts they make, whatever they accomplish, they will never be good enough. A feeling of dissatisfaction about their achievements remains.

The major strategy workaholics employ to placate the harsh demands of their superego is to achieve at work. Hard work turns into a form of redemption. However, although they may experience a sense of relief when they have finished a task, that respite is only temporary. Soon afterward, that nagging feeling of dissatisfaction, anxiety, and insecurity comes back.

For workaholics, self-esteem and work achievement are closely intertwined. All the eggs of self-esteem are in the basket of work. Like children having to cope with overdemanding parents, at work they continue to live under the impression (faulty though it may be) that the "others" will always find fault with them. Although in reality they can be highly effective workers, they feel that they never live up to expectations. So in a compulsive way, they try and try again.

Although we could hail workaholics as the backbone of the work ethic, we may ask ourselves whether their behavior is not ultimately self-defeating. How long can they keep on delivering the goods? Success by that measure can become increasingly difficult as workaholics rise in the organization. How long can they be given short-term, well-defined projects? How long can you keep them out of management functions with less specific goals? What becomes stressful to them, as they climb the organizational ladder, is that the time horizon changes; it takes them longer to show successes. Moreover, there is also such a thing as an organizational funnel; there is less room at the top. With so many people wanting the same goodies, it is not as easy any longer to show tangible achievements and appease the superego.

Furthermore, workaholics may find themselves in a corporate trap: the more they do, the more they are given to do, setting the stage for eventual failure and collapse. They may become so overworked that they become first frustrated and then mentally and physically exhausted; they may eventually run themselves into the ground. Remember, too, that *constant* activity is not the same as *meaningful* activity. The former may turn into plain busywork. Compulsive rituals, such as constantly checking and rechecking whether work has been done correctly, are a good example of this.

The key question is this: What can be done to help these individuals? Is there a way to change the behavior of workaholics? Can we give them a more loving superego?

One of the problems we face in seeking to help workaholics is that (since many of the relevant processes are unconscious) workaholics often lack insight into why they behave as they do. They do not *remember* the reasons. And given their manic way of doing things, they are not the kind of people who take time out for reflection. Frequently, the only kind of memories they have are the emotions that were attached to earlier experiences: feelings of restlessness, dissatisfaction, and anxiety. However, they cannot explain the cause of these feelings. Since much of their behavior is not at a conscious level, it is very hard for workaholics to acknowledge what they are doing to themselves. When confronted with certain aspects of their behavior, they are likely to deny what they are told and go through elaborate rationalization processes.

In view of this, cynics may argue that the best thing that can happen to a workaholic is to suffer a mild coronary. Marcel Proust once said, "Illness is the most heeded of doctors: to goodness and wisdom we only make promises; pain we obey."

Unfortunately, Proust may have been right; physical pain may very well be the only way to stop such people. When their bodies no longer cooperate and they find themselves stuck in a hospital, workaholics may finally allow themselves some time to think.

One of the conditions for change is the acquisition of insight. Workaholics have to learn to remember, in order to rediscover the reasons behind their drive for constant activity. They must learn to articulate their feelings and to become more aware of what they are doing, and why. They must realize that habitual patterns of behavior no longer work very well for them. Without insight into their inner world, however, it is very hard for them to modify their behavior.

Usually, individuals alone are not able to acquire new ways of looking at themselves. They may need the help of a good friend, a spouse, or a colleague or superior at work. In many instances, how-ever, the assistance of a psychotherapist is needed. The therapist, who is in a more neutral position than such associates, can make problems and events more explicit and help the workaholic to real-ize what he or she is doing. This form of therapy can be done indi-vidually or in a group. It is very easy to imagine a support group for workaholics similar to Alcoholics Anonymous.

In psychotherapy, through the process of confrontation and clarification, the problems of workaholism can be brought into greater focus and individuals can gain greater insight into what is happening to them. Unfortunately, insight alone, though vital, is not a sufficient condition for change. Workaholics put up enormous resistance to change. Remember that it takes many years to acquire workaholic behavior patterns. In addition, there may be some kind of secondary gain attached to them. What I mean by this is that a particular dysfunctional behavior, stressful as it may seem, may also give some kind of pleasure, even if only for a short time. Accomplishing an assignment, for example, gives a temporary sense of relief. However, as workaholics well know, the sensation is fleeting.

The workaholic has to learn how to experiment with other modes of functioning. We must not expect an instant, major transformation; it is the little things that count. The workaholic has to be gradually weaned away from his or her dysfunctional mode. Miracles are out of the question; this is not something that is going to happen overnight.

Basically, workaholics have forgotten how to play. They have also lost control over their own lives, having relinquished that control to other people. The transitional space of childhood—a time when there was real wonderment, awe, excitement, and surprise—is completely forgotten. Workaholics can express themselves only through action, engaging in compulsive work behavior with no real pleasure attached.

What workaholics need is to get hold of their own lives; as I have stressed, they have to become more aware of what they are doing to themselves. The first step in this process is to engage in increased self-reflection. Workaholics have to start asking themselves not only what they are running from but also what they are running toward. Are the goals they have set for themselves in life realistic? Do they know their limitations? Have they really paid attention to the way they deal with difficult situations? Have they ever asked themselves how they deal with stress, anxiety, and disappointment? What can they say about the quality of their interpersonal relationships? Do they have people they can turn to for support? Do they take time out to care for others?

Workaholics, by reducing their space for play and thought, have really limited their freedom. They have to go back to basics and explore a different life-style. They have to arrive at a better balance between work and home. This may mean taking time out for leisure; they have to learn how to relax. They have to look for physical and spiritual outlets as well. And last but not least, they have to take some time out for humor. To get out of the rut, they have to make the jump from doing to being. Very likely, in doing so they will gain a better life; these needed changes will make for a more balanced and happier individual. The German playwright Friedrich Schiller seems to have been very aware of this process when he said, "Man only plays when in the full meaning of the word he is a man, and he is only completely a man when he plays." And is it not true that the busiest people have the most leisure?

15

Dead Fish, Incorporated
Alexithymia in Organizations

Ronald Reagan is the triumph of the embalmer's art.
Gore Vidal

Man is only truly great when he acts from his passions.
Benjamin Disraeli

A lan Ayckbourn's play *Man of the Moment*, which was staged a number of years ago at the Globe Theatre in London, is a piece of theater that gives the spectator an uncanny depiction of a particular type of executive sometimes found in organizations. In the play, the audience follows the adventures of Jill Rillington, a TV hostess/producer who is filming her latest TV episode. The basis of this episode is an incident that took place almost two decades earlier, when Vic Parks, now host of a highly successful and popular TV children's show, tried to rob a bank. He was thwarted by one of the bank employees, Douglas Beechey, who had the nerve (or some would say the idiocy) to run up to him in an attempt to take away his gun while he was holding one of the female employees hostage. The gun went off in the struggle, seriously wounding and disfiguring the woman, who later became Beechey's wife.

Rillington's plan is to reunite Beechey with Parks and see what human drama she can get out of it. Thus she organizes a meeting at Parks's luxurious beach house, complete with swimming pool and servants, on the Spanish Riviera. This location contrasts with the modest circumstances in which Beechey lives with his disfigured, now agoraphobic wife. It is Rillington's hope that these contradictions—this situation where the villain ends up so far ahead of the hero—will create some emotional fireworks.

But whatever Rillington tries (and she uses some pretty heavy artillery), nothing seems to unsettle Beechey. His life has a Teflon-like quality: nothing sticks. Everything always seems to be just fine. Rillington makes desperate efforts to get behind the mask, to see if there is something more than this permanent state of blandness, but Beechey continues to spout platitudes. However emotional Rillington's intervention, nothing seems to ruffle Beechey.

Maybe you can imagine Beechey at the bank: slow, plodding, sincere, and without a drop of humor. He is one of those people you would love to shake in order to see if any life comes out. The incident with the bank robber is apparently the only time he has come to life.

Sometimes the label *alexithymic* is given to people like Beechey. You have never heard this description? This is not surprising, because it is a relatively new word. Peter Sifneos, a Boston psychiatrist, coined the term, although two French psychiatrists first identified this mode of functioning.[1] The term comes from the Greek and means literally "no words for emotions." The people we categorize as alexithymics are individuals who show no passion—individuals who, like Beechey, seem to have no fire in their belly.

How do you identify alexithymics? The symptoms include an impoverished fantasy life, a paucity of inner emotional experience, and a tendency toward a lifeless, detail-oriented way of speaking. Winston Churchill's description of the Russian politician Vyacheslav Molotov seems to mark the latter as an alexithymic: "I have never seen a human being who more perfectly represented the modern conception of a robot."

It is very hard to find any life in alexithymics. Their behavior has a kind of mechanical quality. They seem to be unperturbed by what other people would find to be emotionally turbulent experiences. A death in the family, a partner's infidelity, being passed over for promotion, almost being hit by a car—nothing seems to ruffle them. All experience seems to slide down into a black hole of inexpressiveness and blankness. It seems impossible to get any spontaneous reactions from them.

The roots of this disorder—more common among men than women—go back to the earliest years. Some researchers maintain that there is a type of overprotective mother who may frustrate the child's individuality and spirit of adventure, not allowing the child to feel for him- or herself. Such a mother treats her child as an extension of herself and discourages the child's natural emotions. She has, as it were, taken over from the child and become the barometer of his or her emotions.[2]

Does the behavior pattern of alexithymics sound familiar? Have you encountered such people? And how did you react when you met them? Did you feel rather awkward dealing with them?

Large organizations seem to be popular hideaways for such people. Think of all those men in their gray flannel suits who act so politely—the kind of people who seem to make all the right noises. But oh! can they be boring! Noise may come out of them, but there is no music. They are like dead fish. They lack sincerity and genuineness. Interaction with them has a draining quality. You feel like jolting them in order to get some kind of reaction out of them. But despite your efforts to awaken them psychologically, nothing seems to happen. Such people can be exhausting because of their lack of life.

You might decide that if they feel comfortable acting the way they do, that is their business. That may be very true, but are they really healthy individuals? Do they feel comfortable the way they are? The stress symptoms they display often tell a very different story. If you delve deeper, you may find out that they are great somatizers. (They are certainly no strangers to bodily complaints.) There really is something psychologically wrong with them.

Alexithymics do not necessarily act alone. Their behavior—particularly if they have risen to a high position in an organization—may affect others. Having made their typically bland noises, some of them have acquired considerable executive responsibility over time, becoming role models for other executives in the process. And given the charismatic functions of leadership (described in Chapter One)—which include such important elements as energizing and empowering—alexithymic behavior can have ominous implications for organizational effectiveness when these leaders are at the helm.

Unfortunately, many large corporations seem to encourage alexithymic behavior. After all, alexithymics seem to be predictable, and organizations like predictability. Some organizations do not want mavericks around—people who put their neck on the line and carry their heart on their sleeve. They do not like people who rock the boat, who are disturbing and disrupt the routine.

Alexithymics tend to play it safe, and often their behavior seems to pay off. As we have seen, when you make no real decisions, you cannot make mistakes in an organization—an environment where standing out or making bold moves is risky. And the risk aversion of alexithymics is rewarded accordingly. To again adapt Gresham's Law—that bad money drives out good money—mediocrity can drive out excellence.

The corporate culture of certain organizations appears to cultivate alexithymic behavior. In one of my previous books, *Unstable at the Top,* I describe two different types of organization that might do this: the "compulsive" and the "depressive."

The compulsive organization is a highly bureaucratic company that tends to focus inward. A very strict hierarchy is observed. Status derives directly from job title. The leadership tends to dominate the organization from top to bottom and demands strict conformity. Rigid, programmed procedures dominate all aspects of the business and of employer/employee relationships. Walking through various telecommunications organizations, major car manufacturing outfits, insurance companies, and banks can be an eye-opener. Many compulsive organizations can be found in all industries, however. Emotional expressiveness is seldom the strong suit of employees in compulsive organizations.

The depressive organization is even more conservative and maladjusted. The depressive companies I have observed seem to be drifting; they survive only because of various protectionist practices. They have only the vaguest goals, lack strong leadership, and rely on bureaucracy and ritual. Decisions are put off, little effort is made to improve output or standing, and change is viewed with great skepticism. Some now-defunct companies in the steel and machinery industries fit this organizational type very well.

Obviously, executives with an alexithymic disposition feel quite at home in these two types of organization, since the existing corporate culture will be conducive to their kind of behavior. Moreover, some of the nonalexithymic executives may adapt, having discovered that this type of behavior is best for their longevity in the organization. If they do not choose adaptation, most leave voluntarily or are encouraged to leave. For the alexithymically inclined, these types of corporate culture provide ideal holding environments—workplaces in which they are less conspicuous than elsewhere.

Although other types of organization may have a similar quality, none has the kind of numbing effect found in these two. Unfortunately, if organizations are dominated by numb, alexithymic behavior, their life span is going to be limited. They will stagnate, fall into bankruptcy, or (more likely) be taken over.

Let me shift my focus somewhat at this point to look at leaders who possess some of these alexithymic characteristics. Have you ever worked for a "dead fish"? Have you ever had to deal with a person who shows no emotion, who always keeps his or her distance? Such behavior on the part of a leader can contribute to total confusion in an organization. When a boss shows no reaction or demonstrates schizoidlike behavior (is afraid of getting too close), other executives may become confused about what is expected of them and become more interested in power plays than in focusing on the business at hand. The end result is often an atmosphere characterized by conflict and political gamesmanship.

I recall one organization where, due to the extremely detached, unexpressive behavior of the CEO, executives were bewildered about what kind of behavior and action was acceptable. The more competent executives started to leave. Some of the others became increasingly parochial in outlook and engaged in turf wars. The company eventually had to file for bankruptcy. The leader's lack of emotion created in its turn inappropriate emotion, thereby spelling disaster for the company.

In studying this phenomenon, we have to remind ourselves that one of the key roles a senior executive has to play is that of a "container" of the emotions of his or her subordinates. As I mentioned in Chapter One, a good executive has to be something of a psychiatric social worker. Derailment on the road to the top, as I have noted, is usually not the consequence of a lack of technical skills, such as those in marketing, finance, or manufacturing (which are relatively easy to learn), but the consequence of a lack of interpersonal skills. Excellent executives tend to take the emotional pulse of their subordinates on a daily basis. They want to know whether their subordinates feel mad, sad, bad, or glad. Understanding the preoccupations of one's subordinates is a key element in motivating them.

For those who have difficulty in playing this role, there is a ready alternative to human contact. Why talk to people if you can communicate with things! The computer and information revolution and recent advances in telecommunications have been a boon to alexithymics. No wonder there is a ready-made market for each new personal computer and video game. Who needs warmth while interacting with a computer screen? No need to react to verbal and nonverbal signals. Not surprisingly, many alexithymics have found a haven in the data-processing field. "Systems people" concern themselves with work of an impersonal nature: their contacts with other people are depersonalized, mechanical, and frequently intellectual. These people carry out fixed routines and procedures and deal in abstractions, thereby abolishing real relationships with real people. Feelings become superfluous.

In this portrait gallery, we should not leave out the pretenders—people who appear to show emotions but in fact lack true conviction, real warmth, and sincerity. They play the role of a "welcome wagon," but their compulsive sociability is symptomatic of their inability to show real concern. The mask of extroversion becomes a disguise for the emptiness of their inner theater.

Since such persons have a hard time really feeling (just as color-blind people have trouble distinguishing colors), they need others to tell them how to feel. There is a chameleon-like quality to alexithymics' ability to pick up signals from the outside world and adjust their behavior accordingly.

Have you traveled on one of the large airlines lately? Remember the big smile of welcome and the hearty greeting—"Have a nice day!"—you received? This may be better than a hostile glare and surly treatment, but do you ever wonder what goes on underneath, what those smiling flight attendants *really* feel? Would you not think they are sometimes tempted, after the thousandth "Have a nice day," to say, "Buzz off"—or something rather worse? I should hope so, for their sake, although acting on that urge would not endear them to the company, of course.

Actually, some companies that pride themselves on being customer-friendly, including the Disney Corporation, have inspectors around to make sure that such a breakdown in communication—an outburst like the hypothetical one I mentioned above—does not take place. Every employee has to undergo a thorough indoctrination process that one might be excused for thinking of as brainwashing. Elaborate manuals are used to point out what behavior is appropriate on what occasions. These companies want their employees to show the right emotions at the right time, irrespective of their mood. However, this form of emotional management may in the long run carry a hefty pricetag in terms of alienation, depersonalization, depression, and other disorders.

In spite of what some organizations seem to prefer, the man in the gray flannel suit should not be an ideal type. The costs are just too high, not only for the individual but also for the organization. For the purposes of mental health, it is necessary for executives to show a degree of authenticity in the expression of their feelings. Given the position of authority they occupy, senior executives are powerful role models. They have a responsibility to demonstrate that they themselves are alive, that they appreciate impassioned statements, and that the expression of emotions will not have negative consequences for a person's career. Fulfilling that responsibility is what makes people such as Jack Welch, Richard Branson, and Sir John Harvey Jones true business heroes. These thoroughly nonalexithymic leaders are not afraid to put their feelings and emotions up front.

The comedian Groucho Marx once said of someone, "Either this man is dead or my watch has stopped." Funny though this comment may be, if it describes your organization, you had better think seriously about how to clear out the dead fish that are polluting the environment.

16

· ·

Doing a Maxwell

The Dark Side of Entrepreneurship

He'll charm the birds off the trees and then shoot them.[1]
Union leader Bill Keyes about Robert Maxwell

Entrepreneurs are the lifeblood of business, but as leaders they are also susceptible to excess. Entrepreneurs often behave outrageously, and a more colorful illustration than the late Robert Maxwell would be hard to find.

It was in all the newspapers; there is no way you could have missed it. All the elements of a detective story were there. While cruising on his yacht off the Canary Islands, a famous business tycoon drowns under mysterious circumstances. Accident, suicide, or foul play? The autopsy verdict, which mentions both heart trouble and drowning, seems inconclusive. The result of it all? A sprawling global communications empire—the Mirror Group Newspapers and Maxwell Communications Corporation—falls apart!

That was the scenario, but there was more to come. Soon after his death, the late "socialist multimillionaire" was accused of being the "crook of the century." It turned out that he had been using his various companies' pension funds to shore up the shaky price of his shares. In doing so, he apparently defrauded his companies of at least $1.4 billion. More than twenty-five banks and investment firms were caught red-faced and struggled to make sense of the financial quagmire. A rags to riches story turned sour; a Greek tragedy in contemporary times.

In retrospect, we can ask ourselves what went on in Maxwell's mind while he was on his yacht, *Lady Ghislaine*. Did he know that his days were numbered? He must have been aware, certainly, of the fact that his companies were in a downward spin. There were several loans to be paid back. (As a matter of fact, on the day of his death he had promised the immediate redemption of a $100 million loan to the Swiss Bank Corporation.) Would he have been able to put off his creditors much longer? How long could he have continued robbing Peter to pay Paul? Was he aware that the game was over?

To many, Robert Maxwell came across as larger than life. Certainly, he was a man of great contrasts and contradictions. His life story is the stuff adventure novels are made of. And despite all his wrongdoings, Maxwell was undeniably a man of remarkable courage and energy.

Abraham Lajbi Hoch, alias Robert Maxwell (he changed his name three times during the course of his life) was born in 1923 of Jewish parents in the Slovakian peasant village of Solotvino. His family was extremely poor; there was rarely enough to eat (which may partially explain Maxwell's obsession with food later on). His education came to an end after only three years, because he was too poorly clothed to go to school. However, in spite of all their difficulties, the Hochs were a close family, and Abraham was his mother's favorite, a very important aspect of his childhood.

Maxwell grew up in a period of great upheaval: Czechoslovakia would become one of the first countries to fall victim to Hitler's expansionist plans. Maxwell's family saw the perils threatening the household and managed to send him, at sixteen, to Budapest and away from immediate danger. Maxwell was the sole member of his family to survive the concentration camps. His being a survivor may very well have contributed to his ruthlessness, drive, determination, and exceptional sense of purpose. These are characteristics often observed in people who, having had a new lease on life, become— to use psychologist William James's description—"twice born."

Maxwell fought briefly with Czech forces in France before being evacuated to England. He returned to the continent with the British Army, was awarded the Military Cross for bravery in action, and was later promoted to the rank of captain. He became British through naturalization and then, toward the end of the war, married Elisabeth Meynard, a French Protestant with whom he later had nine children (seven survive). At the time of their marriage, he prophesied that he would become a millionaire and a Member of Parliament. Years later, he would indeed become a Labour MP, a strong supporter of the ideals of democratic socialism.

As an executive, Maxwell became hugely successful. In postwar Germany, he recognized the great potential for power and profit that could be realized in the information business. This led to the creation of the cornerstone of his empire, Pergamon Press, which published scientific literature. Over time, Maxwell succeeded in transforming this profitable but rather unglamorous printing and publishing business into a sprawling, highly visible global media empire. Because of his talents in aggressive turnaround management, he is considered to have been highly instrumental in restructuring the British printing industry.

But there were clouds on the horizon throughout the buildup of his empire. Many individuals had been rubbed the wrong way by Maxwell's way of doing business. Although he could be quite charming when he needed something, he had a very abrasive personality. His aggression frightened people. Many also had serious doubts about his business ethics. The shorthand term "the Max factor" was coined, indicating that shares in Maxwell's companies traded lower than they would have done if someone else had been in charge.

There may have been good reasons for a number of these concerns. Some people recalled how the London financial establishment had condemned Maxwell's behavior early in his career, stating that he was not "a person who can be relied upon to exercise proper stewardship of a publicly-quoted company." This statement was the conclusion of the report by the London stock market's watchdog committee after an investigation centered on the sale of Pergamon

Press. It was a verdict that would haunt him throughout his business career.

The investigation had been triggered by the purchaser's complaint that he had been misled about the true value of Pergamon. The committee's report, published on June 2, 1971, said that Maxwell's statements to shareholders showed "a reckless and unjustified optimism" that sometimes led him "to state what he must have known to be untrue." The report was particularly damning in regard to the way in which Maxwell had inflated the sales of his Pergamon encyclopedia unit by selling to an American subsidiary that was part of his holdings.

Considering everything that was known about Maxwell, and the way in which he built up his empire, it is interesting to ask how he managed to get away with all he did in the years after the committee's report. How could things have gone so far? Did nobody ever consider that "the bouncing Czech," as he was called, might fall back on his old tricks when under stress? Was he really a reformed man?

Numerous people must have been in a position to blow the whistle on Maxwell over the years. He had loaded the boards of the Mirror Group Newspapers and Maxwell Communications Corporation with London and Whitehall worthies. What had all these bigwigs been doing? Their specific mandate was to be watchdogs for the various stakeholders in his companies; yet not one expressed concern about the way Maxwell was managing. Were they bullied into silence? Were they somewhat confused about all the different dealings in which Maxwell was involved and reluctant to admit that they could make no sense of the maze of interlocking companies making up his empire? Since the bulk of Maxwell's private holdings was kept in secret family trusts in Gibraltar and Liechtenstein, they might not have been able to discern the boundaries between what was privately held and what was publicly held. Still, it must have been clear that he was juggling public and private assets. The published year-end earnings of Maxwell's empire in March 1991 were obviously convoluted, coming mostly from currency trading and not from the results of core business. Did no one perceive that, in a frantic effort to solve his cash-flow problems, Maxwell was trying to make money through currency transactions—and was losing his shirt in the process?

It should not have come as much of a surprise that Maxwell's empire collapsed with debts amounting to almost $4.4 billion. Yet no one had warned him that many of his acquisitions were greatly overpriced. No one had seemed worried about the level of his debt load. He was known to have paid $3.35 billion for Macmillan and Official Airline Guides in 1988, and at the time most sources agreed that the buyout was anything but a bargain. This was followed by his highly costly but failed bid for Harcourt Brace Jovanovich, investments in Eastern Europe, purchases of television stations in France and Israel, and a hodgepodge of acquisitions (including newspapers and news agencies and computer, helicopter, and pharmaceutical companies). All in all, Maxwell's holdings amounted to more than 400 businesses worldwide at the time of his death.[2]

Yet executives at a host of financial institutions backed Maxwell's wildly ambitious, often unrealistic plans. They ignored his checkered reputation and kept on financing him. Were they really gullible, or were they merely blinded by greed? It is now obvious that the financial institutions involved will probably lose up to $2 billion in the Maxwell affair. It is true that banks caught up in the merger and acquisition frenzy in the eighties were ready to back any mad idea. Furthermore, Maxwell was known to be one of the most litigious people in England, famous for his ability to sue any critic into silence. But are these reasons adequate to explain what happened?

One factor that has received insufficient attention is the extent to which Maxwell's personality affected his surroundings. What kind of psychological dynamics were at work in and around him as he made his way up?

In many ways, Maxwell was a typical entrepreneur. This is not a pejorative statement; there are many good things to be said about entrepreneurs. Entrepreneurs are the driving force of any country's economy; they represent the wealth of a nation and its potential to create employment. Entrepreneurs are the people who make things happen, the ones who come up with new ideas and put them into action, the ones who provide the enthusiasm and sense of purpose that empower others. Unfortunately, there can also be a darker side to their behavior. Many entrepreneurs possess personality quirks that, while originally a source of great strength, can—when excessive—lead to their downfall.

Let me explain what I mean. First of all, many entrepreneurs have a very ambivalent attitude toward control. They are afraid of being at the mercy of others. More than most people, they want to be in charge. Some entrepreneurs may want to be informed about even the most minute details of what goes on in their organization. What may have been all right for a mom-and-pop operation, however, has no place in a multi-million-dollar enterprise. For example, I remember talking to the president of a $15 million operation who still insisted on opening all the mail. This may have been a good policy when the company was in its infancy, but wasting one's energy on these things at a later stage in the company's life cycle is indicative of a certain pathology.

Many entrepreneurs have difficulty addressing issues of dominance and submission. Authority figures raise entrepreneurial hackles. Structured situations are alien to such executives unless they are the ones who created the structure in the first place. They like things to be done on their terms. Some even create a corporate culture that prohibits any form of contrarian thinking. In such a culture, disagreement is impossible; there is no tolerance for subordinates who think for themselves; give-and-take—the process of real dialogue—is not permitted.

Maxwell demonstrated quite a few of these characteristics. He was resistant to advice from others. In his companies, there was only one way of doing things. It was his way or the highway. He was anything but a good listener. He had to control everything around him, whether people or companies. He knew only one kind of relation-ship: master and slave. In Maxwell's organizations, board meetings were a joke. Maxwell intimidated board members, making them afraid to offer their input. He would even go so far as to force a board to delegate all power to him—a rather crude way of getting rid of board meetings altogether. Maxwell used these bulldozer tac-tics to get his own way.

Subordinates had to carry out Maxwell's instructions to the let-ter. He expected total obedience. When he said, "Jump," the only acceptable response was, "How high?" It was out of the question to query his instructions. His need for control sometimes led him to hire capable people, give them impressive titles, and then not allow them to do the job. Instead, he would do it himself. Being hired by Maxwell meant the end of having any influence over him. Every-thing, however trivial it might be, had to be approved by Maxwell—which certainly did not speed up the decision-making process.

Maxwell's strong need for control was also reflected in the highly secret world he created around his private companies. Because secrecy and security were prime concerns, Maxwell had a passion for security devices. He even had the phones of his fellow directors of the Mirror Group Newspapers bugged—without their knowledge, of course. He also installed a public-address system through which he could berate his employees. Furthermore, only Maxwell himself had any idea about all the links between his myriad companies. There was no manage-ment structure; everything revolved around and depended on him. Through this kind of fragmentation, which created a considerable amount of obscurity, he kept control over all decisions.

This secret world Maxwell had created to maintain his control brings us to another characteristic of some entrepreneurs: their dis-trust of others. Some entrepreneurs live in fear of being victimized and feel best when their fortunes are at their lowest. Like many other people who find themselves at the top of the heap, they dread the envy of others and thus become anxious when successful. Their anx-iety may actually abate somewhat when their anticipated downfall has occurred. Then they have paid off their psychological debt (the unconscious guilt they feel about their success) and can start anew. This may partially explain why so many entrepreneurs have a re-markable capacity to bounce back. If we look at the ups and downs of Maxwell's career, he falls perfectly into this category: the bouncing Czech succeeded in surviving for a very long time.

When a strong feeling of distrust is combined with a need for control, the consequences for the organization can be serious. Para-noid thinkers will always find some form of reality, some kind of real danger out there. It is always possible to confirm the belief that there is somebody out to get you. In an organizational culture that fosters such thinking, people may stop acting independently, allow-ing sycophancy and political gamesmanship to become rampant. Since even harmless acts may be interpreted as threats and lead to violent explosions, many people start to play it safe and stop making decisions. An organization with this sort of culture will never grow and adapt.

Maxwell built just this sort of culture into his organization. He was a specialist in "mushroom treatment," by which people are kept in the dark. As Peter Jay, once a top executive in the Maxwell empire, said about his former boss's management philosophy, "Things were run on a need-to-know principle: if you needed to know, you were not told."[3] When people in the company asked questions, they were very quickly excluded from the information flow. In this context, Maxwell's regularly overheard appeal—"Trust me!"—acquired ironic overtones.

Another characteristic frequently found among entrepreneurs is their great desire for applause. One way of interpreting this is as a narcissistic reaction against feelings of insignificance—the fear of being considered a nobody. Some entrepreneurs seem to be con-stantly haunted by an inner voice telling them that they have not amounted to anything. To make up for the feelings that result, they have a strong urge to prove the world wrong. They are going to get even, have a vindictive triumph, and make it to the top in spite of all the forces against them. Their need to compensate for wrong-doings done to them (real or imagined) becomes an overpowering force. This unhealthy type of narcissism may well have been a contributing factor in Maxwell's incredible drive.

Maxwell was indefatigable in seeking (and getting) attention. Roy Greenslade, a former *Daily Mirror* top editor (fired), once said that "[Maxwell's] ego was bigger than Saddam Hussein's. Maxwell was a one-man circus: juggler, conjurer, publicity agent."[4] He constantly needed an entourage and an audience. But the audience could be kept waiting; he rarely had the courtesy to be on time. The hallway in front of his office was always jammed with people waiting to see him.

Maxwell was infamous as a self-promoter and was irrepressibly boastful. The entry under his name in the 1990 edition of *Who's Who* (an entry that he wrote himself) runs over forty-five lines and includes such tidbits as a 1983 award from Bulgaria.

Much of Maxwell's behavior indicates that he wanted to create a monument to glorify his achievements. He wanted to paint his "M" logo all over the globe, both literally and figuratively. His objective was to be in the news constantly, even at the price of creating a bloated empire. The *Daily Mirror* was turned into a kind of family album, with Maxwell writing his own headlines. He constantly badgered financial writers from other newspapers into covering his activities as well. He also acquired a soccer club, another highly effective way to stay in the public eye.

Maxwell's nemesis appears to have been Keith Rupert Murdoch. During much of his life, Maxwell seemed to be in a race with this other media baron, a man who regularly frustrated Maxwell's ambitions by outbidding him for such newspapers as the *Sun*, the *News of the World*, and the *Times*. These bidding wars led to the acquisition by Maxwell of a number of very flashy but financially fragile media properties. His final touch in this race was the acquisition of yet another newspaper, the *Daily News*. His insatiability forced him to leverage his companies to the hilt and eventually led to financial ruin.

Entrepreneurs also resort to some peculiarly primitive defensive processes, which can lead to a great discrepancy between the narrative truth and the historical truth: facts are arranged to suit the individual's needs. Observers of Maxwell could not help but notice the contradictions between what he said and what he did. More and more people began to realize that Maxwell had a very idiosyncratic way of interpreting facts.

Splitting—a behavior pattern whereby everything is seen in extremes: black or white, friend or foe—is a defense mechanism often used by entrepreneurs. This was the case with Maxwell, certainly. If you disagreed with him, you were his enemy. He did not take easily to different points of view. He was not a person to forgive or forget his enemies' "crimes." On the contrary, he had a memory like an elephant and would go to great lengths to get even.

Some entrepreneurs also have a tendency to blame others for what goes wrong. Scapegoating is an excellent way of blaming others while feeling virtuous oneself. Maxwell clearly demonstrated this behavior pattern. He never found fault with his own actions and was quick to blame others for mistakes. People could be reduced to trembling wrecks by his anger.

In order to assign blame elsewhere, entrepreneurs may rationalize away whatever responsibility they have for questionable events. Their capacity to delude themselves can be tremendous. There is always an explanation for things, however convoluted. Certainly, Maxwell was a person who would often stretch his own credibility in explaining the reasons for his actions.

Certain entrepreneurs are incapable of sitting still. This originates in the difficulty many of them have in controlling their impulses and managing anxiety and depression. Everything we know about Maxwell points to the fact that he was a dynamo, a real wheeler-dealer, anything but a man able to take things easy. He was constantly on the move, by Concorde, helicopter, limousine, or yacht, and was constantly talking on the telephone. He was an excessively action-oriented individual.

In the end, where does the story of Maxwell leave us? Should we merely close the case by quoting Lord Acton and say, "Power corrupts, and absolute power corrupts absolutely"? Should we conclude that power leads to excessive narcissistic behavior, with all its repercussions: grandiose fantasies, boastful and pretentious behavior, arrogance, feelings of entitlement, and self-centeredness? Or perhaps we should look at the Maxwell drama as a cautionary tale that emphasizes the need to have counterbalancing powers in society and organizations. As we have seen, the psychological pressures that are brought to bear on leaders can easily lead them astray. Many become blinded to the true consequences of their actions.

In Maxwell's case, the countervailing forces did not work very well. The regulators dealing with pension funds were not vigilant. The city of London, with its myriad bankers, stockbrokers, and investment analysts, failed to act. Furthermore, the many members of Maxwell's various boards never executed their function properly, whether for reasons of greed, collective delusion, or plain stupidity. The same can be said about the role that the various public accountancy firms played.

None of this clears Maxwell, of course. It was his responsibility (as it is for every top executive) to do some preventive maintenance himself. A more astute leader would have taken time out for reflection, would have recognized ethical boundaries. Such a person would have been more aware of the repercussions of his or her particular leadership style: how it would negatively affect organizational functioning. The astute leader would have created a different ambience—one that allowed other people's voices to be heard. If Maxwell had done these things, it is unlikely that he would have found himself in the predicament he did. The looser ambience might have made him less gluttonous and allowed him a fuller and even happier life. Perhaps he should have heeded the advice of General Eisenhower, who said, "You do not lead by hitting people over the head—that's assault, not leadership." But given Maxwell's background, the frontal assault may have been the only approach that came naturally.

17

Why Work for a Genghis Khan?
Appeasing the Aggressor

Right in the middle of Prague, Wenceslaus Square,
there's this guy throwing up. And this other guy
comes along, takes a look at him, shakes his head,
and says, "I know just what you mean."

Milan Kundera

My mother . . . had made herself, or acquired, a little
figurine called Ronnie, Ronald, that she was sticking
pins in, its head you know, to give me a heart attack.

Ronald Laing

When studying the personality and business practices of a leader such as Robert Maxwell, an obvious question arises: Why do some managers continue to work for bosses who behave like Genghis Khan—continually heaping abuse on their subordinates, humiliating them, and blaming them for things they did not do or even think of doing? What makes for followership beyond the call of duty? As we saw with Robert Maxwell, the Genghis Khans of the corporate world are never satisfied; whatever is achieved, it is not good enough. These organizational bullies are exploitative, overcontrolling, sadistic, and abrasive. Not only do they present a very tough, domineering, power-oriented façade; they can also be very dogmatic, strongly opinionated, and dangerously narrow-minded. These tyrants of the business world have an exceedingly foul temper—one that flares up readily. Because being quarrelsome is part and parcel of their makeup, they are very unpleasant people to be with.

Remember Leona Helmsley, the self-anointed queen of the Helmsley hotel empire? She acquired more notoriety for her brutality toward the people who worked for her than for her talent for tax evasion (which eventually landed her in jail). The "Lady Macbeth of the lodging industry" (as the *New York Times* once called her) knew how to act as a petty tyrant better than anyone else. And consider Robert Abbout, who has had a long and stormy career as a banker and financier. He gained notoriety and a place on *Fortune* magazine's hit parade of America's ten toughest bosses because of his aggressive, truculent style as president of First Chicago Corporation and Occidental Petroleum, before deciding ("helped" by various stakeholders in these companies) to run his own investment company. His ability to emasculate his people through his abrasiveness and meddling has become famous throughout the banking fraternity.

Have you ever met or worked with the kind of people I am talking about? Do you recognize embryonic Maxwells, Helmsleys, and Abbouts in your organization, even if they are not classed in the same league of champions?

There are a lot of these people around. The mystery is why certain executives continue to work for them—for bosses who never show a sign of gratitude for a job well done, who seem to mete out nothing but ill-treatment. It is a puzzle why some people subject themselves to bosses who behave in such an insensitive, abusive, and controlling manner. Why don't these people either take a stand or get out? What makes for the extremes of followership? As I pointed out earlier, life is not a rehearsal. Merely hanging in there is self-defeating. To continue working for such people, under difficult circumstances, seems rather pathological, given that the only memorable quality of these abusive employers seems to be their capacity to inflict pain. (I realize that people who decide to work for a particular executive may not be aware in advance what they are in for; they may be astonished to find themselves with an abusive boss. Most of these people, however, if they have any sense, soon leave for better things.)

In the clinical literature, we can find certain character descriptions that may shed light on why people are willing to work for someone like Robert Maxwell. Here I am referring to dependent, but particularly masochistic, personality types. People with such personality structures seem to be willing to accept what working for abrasive bosses entails. It is clear that such individuals were more likely to give in to Maxwell, throwing their lot in with the aggressor. In contrast, executives who were not willing to toe the line, who stood up to him, were quickly pushed aside or pushed out. Meanwhile, subordinates willing to play the rule of sycophant would, at times, resort to using Maxwell's aggressive tactics with others. Naturally, such behavior added to the climate of fear.

It is not surprising that many capable executives left Maxwell's organization—particularly those from acquired companies staffed by people unfamiliar with Maxwell's peculiar leadership practices. Many among those who stayed, however, may have felt quite comfortable with the company's culture, coming to view Maxwell's behavior as normal.

People who decide to stay in companies run by such leaders may also have been drawn into an unusual kind of group process that I have described elsewhere as folie à deux. Folie à deux is a strange process that culminates in the creation of a closed community—one in which a sense of reality gradually disappears and in which practices that would be considered questionable or even irrational in other companies go unchallenged.

Psychiatrists sometimes use the term "mental contagion" to describe this peculiar phenomenon. Whatever label it is given, folie à deux essentially involves the sharing of a "delusional" system by two or more individuals. What seems to happen is that a person experiences an attachment to someone else—the dominant person—so intense that it totally overwhelms the affected individual's other behavior patterns, to the detriment of rational thought and reality testing.

Leaders such as Maxwell create an ambience that facilitates folie à deux. In such a situation, subordinates are drawn into supporting the boss in spite of irrational practices that prevail in the organization. Highly abrasive behavior on the part of the leader, such as could be observed in the case of Maxwell, may lead to regression and feelings of helplessness in others, encouraging this unhealthy interaction. Hoarding information, keeping secrets, playing favorites, and inconsistently handling company policies all add to the downward spiral. As people in such situations feel increasingly powerless and vulnerable, they paradoxically cling to the aggressor, whom they also see as a protector.

Many of the people around Maxwell seem to have been willing to sacrifice reality and rational decision making for the "reward" of being accepted by him. It seems they would have done anything in order to ingratiate themselves and preserve their tie to him. We have seen the consequences such behavior had on his empire.

Although this particular work relationship—aggressor and willing follower—may mystify us, as with so many other things that at first glance seem totally puzzling there is a logic behind it. For most of us, though, it may be hard to see that logic, to understand why some individuals appear to be resigned to enduring suffering as a necessary prerequisite for getting the attention of the person who inflicts pain on them.

Some of the individuals we are dealing with here have great difficulties in experiencing pleasure. As mentioned earlier, a strong masochistic predisposition forms part of the psychological makeup of such people. They noticeably fail to show satisfaction in both major achievements and the little pleasures of life. It is almost as if these individuals (consciously or unconsciously) seek mental states of pain; they seem to possess a desire for suffering and exhibit a proclivity toward self-defeating behavior. They appear to lack a clear sense of their own power and initiative. They repeatedly hand over control of their life to others in the hope that somehow these others will compensate for their own deficiencies.

Paradoxically, such people seem to like what is happening to them. They appear to welcome the abuse heaped upon them. Not that they would *show* their enjoyment: heaven forbid! Their attitude is more one of resignation. The best way of typifying their behavior is to say that they are caught in the vicious circle of a self-defeating form of loving. Their actions give us the strong impression that the oppressive presence of another is required for any experience of vitality and wholeness.

These people seem to like being neglected, punished, or made to feel guilty. They feel that they can get another person's attention only through self-negation, submission, and suffering. As a result, they engage in excessive forms of self-sacrifice that appear to be unsolicited. Closer observation may reveal that they actively choose people and situations that predictably lead to disappointment, failure, or mistreatment (although this is not necessarily a conscious process on their part). Often they appear to reject or render ineffective the attempts of others to help them. Instead, they seem to be attracted to people who punish in one way (and therefore gratify in another).

Their relationships to others are characterized by deference, servility, and obsequiousness; they like to ingratiate themselves. To receive any form of attention or help themselves, however, seems to be most unwelcome. As might be expected, this kind of behavior invites exploitation and abuse.

To all appearances, these people enjoy putting themselves in an inferior light. They solicit condemnation by accepting undeserved blame and unjust criticism. In interactions with others, they seem to dwell on their own worst features. Opportunities for pleasure are turned down. As a matter of fact, they are reluctant to acknowledge that there is such a thing as having a good time. Having pleasure or receiving help are things such individuals have difficulty dealing with.

In addition, these individuals find it hard to accept praise. In fact, on the rare occasions they receive praise, it is taken with suspicion. And rightly so, if their boss is an organizational bully from whom favors are fleeting. Praise is seen as a sort of booby trap: these people suspect that they are being set up and wonder when the trapdoor is going to open under them.

Unfortunately, only the experience of pain seems to give such people a sense of connectedness. Some of them seem to be truly alive only when they are being hurt. To make hurt (and therefore life) happen, they may even engage in self-sabotage, inviting negative responses. There seems to be an overriding need for punishment. As someone once told me, "I feel only when I'm being hurt!"

When they are in conflict with a boss, these people blame themselves. They court unjust criticism and accept undeserved blame. They seem incapable of realizing that the other party may be at fault. They may even try to rationalize or deny whatever callous acts their superior commits. It is almost as if they say to themselves each time Genghis Khan goes off the deep end, "Poor thing, he doesn't know what he's doing; he's not really responsible." Given their particular mindset, it is hard to get these people to see what is being done to them. They are very reluctant to accept the true nature of things.

For these martyrs of the corporate world, suffering becomes the preferred form of relating. In their view, a painful relationship is better than no relationship at all. What these people seem to fear most is loneliness and abandonment. They are scared to death of being left out. Thus the pain they receive while suffering in the relationship seems preferable to the pain they believe they would feel if the relationship were to end. Self-sacrifice and abasement become their way of getting closer to others. Paradoxically, these people may even be bored or repelled by people who treat them well.

It should be borne in mind, however, that although these people may appear to be overtly pleasing, self-deprecating, and self-sacrificing, inwardly they are often willful, ambivalent, defiant, and angry. In most instances, however, they seem unaware of any anger they might experience as a result of their relationships. Any strongly negative emotions remain at an unconscious level. When confronted with evidence of what is being done to them by an organizational bully, they have a hard time accepting the anger in themselves. In spite of all the indignities they are exposed to, they prefer to ignore what is happening to them.

One of their favorite roles in organizations is that of caretaker, one who is helpful. This role makes them ideal victims of the Genghis Khans. Deep down, however, their choice of this role may represent a wish to be taken care of as they care for others, and the role itself may give them a sense of vicarious gratification. Indeed, these martyrs prefer this way of relating to asking others for something. By caring for others, they at least experience a sense of control in the process of giving. Owning up to their own dependency needs, and expressing their own desires, makes them feel vulnerable. Furthermore, in their innermost self they believe that they are loved more for what they do than for what they are.

But how does this kind of behavior develop in the first place? What makes these people interact in such a peculiarly self-defeating manner? Where did they learn these behavior patterns? Who influenced them? As usual, when examining strange behavior patterns, we have to go back in time and trace their developmental history.

In many instances, these martyrs were brought up in a very unpredictable environment—one characterized by ambivalent emotional attachment and parental inconsistency and insensitivity. "Do as I say, not as I do" seems to be the first rule in these families. In addition, the parents tend to be dominant, overcontrolling, and extremely intrusive, failing to respect their children's emotional space. Rationality and self-control are not among their virtues. These parents may both punish and reward their children for the same behavior at different times. Likewise, clinging and hitting may occur simultaneously. This leads to considerable confusion on a child's part about how to behave.

The parents of such masochistically inclined people tend to be self-centered. Their responses to their children are based more upon their own needs and demands than upon the needs or wishes of each developing child. Such parents are highly insensitive and are certainly not well equipped to prepare their children to function as adults.

They cause an enormous amount of damage by exploiting their children to cater to their own needs at a time when the developing offspring are very vulnerable. The children quickly become over-burdened and victimized, yet their parents are never satisfied; whatever a child does, it is never good enough. The result of such defective childrearing is a form of anxious attachment. Proper separation and individuation (important for autonomous functioning later on) never occur.

The situation can be aggravated by a sadomasochistic element in the marriage of these parents, with the wife most often cast in the role of victim and the husband in the role of aggressor. This kind of marital role model, presented at an impressionable age, may invite imitation, since it is perceived by the child as normal. Internalization processes being what they are, there is a high probability of imitation and identification with an inadequate or disparaged parent.

Children try to maintain a conception of their parents as good and loving, however, and they therefore attribute any problem in their parents' relationship to faults in themselves. They deny that their parents may have something to do with the prevailing dysfunctional relationship. Confronting that possibility would be devastating to an already very fragile self-concept. It could lead—or so the children think—to the thing every child fears most: abandonment. Painful closeness is better than separation. Given this convoluted way of thinking, children's first thought (regardless of who has in fact contributed to the problem) is always that *they* must be at fault.

In this context, we have to remember the essential inequality of children's position in a family: they are completely dependent on their parents. As dependents, they actively respond to the parents' cues. The type of parents we are talking about give distorted cues that lead to considerable suffering later on. To understand the dynamics that occur, we should also bear in mind that, in children who are growing and learning in these dysfunctional families, certain types of maladaptive response patterns prevail. Why? Because the reward for maladaptive responses comes immediately, while the damage occurs only after considerable delay. Learning experiments have shown us that the immediate gratification of a need tends to have a much stronger effect than deferred pain—even if the long-term pain is much greater than the short-term gratification.

Another factor that fosters the development of this peculiar way of relating to others is the parents' masterly use of such defenses as denial, displacement, reaction-formation, projection, and rationalization. These parents have a knack for externalizing and scapegoating others for whatever wrongs they have done while absolving themselves of fault. With this kind of influence, it is to be expected that their children, who are in fact martyrs in training, prefer to blame themselves for imagined or real wrongdoings. They quickly realize that acting in such a way will please their parents. The parents, on the other hand, give no thought to the pain this pattern of behavior will cause a developing child in the long run. They do not recognize the devastating effect this kind of parenting can have.

The price of this permanent wish to please the aggressor may be the loss of a well-balanced personal identity. For people exposed to this kind of parenting, the equilibrium between dominant and submissive behavior has been lost. They react inappropriately in relationships with others, having acquired a slave mentality. Because as children they vehemently denied that their parents could be at fault, and because their parents were masters at putting the blame on others, a certain amount of complementarity of "master-slave" roles developed—a pattern that is likely to repeat itself in adult life.

Given this kind of background, it should not come as a great surprise that in later life these people persist in loving those who give nothing in return. They seem to search out the Genghis Khans of this world, believing that these abusive leaders—unpleasant though they may be—can do no wrong. In acting the way they do, adult martyrs seem to be motivated by the desire to heal their wounded self-esteem by trying to make their critical or rejecting parents (now replaced by corporate tyrants) love and approve of them. They feel a strong urge to repeat a rather doomed scenario. The expectation is that through these Genghis Khans, they will obtain the closeness they never had while growing up. The possession of such an inner script of pain and surrender (which at one point was imposed on them) goes a long way toward explaining why such people seem to be attracted to individuals who mistreat them. Their inner theater is now enacted on a public stage.

As part of this process, all the natural aggression felt toward the aggressor becomes repressed. In a way, the behavior of adult martyrs can be compared to that of a dog that seems to be even more affectionate and devoted after a beating. Punishment becomes attractive as a way of curbing one's own aggressiveness. Furthermore, by provoking punishment, martyrs create the illusion of magical control over the aggressor.

Given their developmental history, these people seem to be particularly attracted to individuals with rather narcissistic personality constellations—a central characteristic of organizational bullies. They recognize in these bullies the narcissistic supplies in which they themselves are deficient and for which they have been looking all their life. If they can only be sufficiently ingratiating (they believe), they will finally get what they have always wanted. With the Genghis Khans of the world, they are trying to relive and mend their previously unsatisfactory relationships.

This way of behaving serves two functions. Not only does it create an illusion of powerfulness (through the process of identification); it also becomes a way of satisfying the victim's own repressed aggression—in other words, a form of aggression by proxy.

Now that we have some understanding of the form of pleasure these martyrs get out of their martyrdom, what should we advise them to do? Should we just let them be? After all, they do fulfill a role, self-defeating though it may be. They are the ideal audience for the corporate tyrants of the world. There seems to be a perfect complementarity. Everybody is happy in his or her own way: masters need slaves, and slaves need masters.

We should ask ourselves, however, whether this kind of relationship makes for effective organizations. How does master-slave behavior affect organizational culture? Can such relationships really improve performance? Serious doubts must be raised about these issues. Abrasiveness and obsequiousness do not rate highly as keys to success in business leadership. *Fortune* magazine's list of America's toughest bosses is not the Hall of Fame most people would like to find themselves in. Moreover, in most instances, the stories of the people on this list do not have a happy ending. Excellence in organizations requires something other than abrasiveness. It requires the ability to trust others. It requires empowerment. It requires encouraging debate, tolerating mistakes, and taking worthwhile risks. Abrasiveness makes other people *less* effective, and so does obsequiousness; thus they run counter to excellence.

Running organizations is all about getting the best out of people. Under certain circumstances, abrasiveness may get results faster than civility, but usually only in the short term. After all, what kind of legacy have people such as Robert Maxwell left behind?

So where do *you* stand? Do you fit the profile? Are you the sort of person who is constantly being abused? If so, it is high time to get your bags packed. For your own mental health, it is advisable to experiment with other behavior patterns. It may be difficult to make this change alone, so find someone to help you. I realize that achieving a fundamental change such as this will not be easy, but it can be done. The greatest incentive is that the change will make for a much happier life.

There is a joke circulating (albeit very quietly) in Baghdad—a joke about Saddam Hussein, a leader from whom Genghis Khan could learn a few things. It goes something like this: Saddam Hussein is trying to figure out how far he can push his citizens. He starts off by declaring that from now on, every Iraqi has to work sixteen hours a day. Nobody protests; people do as they are told. His next decree is that people will be paid only half the usual sum for their work. Still people obey. Saddam Hussein is rather surprised by this lack of reaction on the part of his citizens and decides to go one step further. He now dictates that soldiers will be posted on each of Baghdad's bridges with explicit orders to give a lashing to each resident crossing the bridge on the way to work. Finally, he gets a reaction. A citizens' committee asks to meet with him. "Great leader," they say, "the beatings make us come late to work. Would it be possible to post more soldiers on the bridges to expedite the beatings?"

The gangster Al Capone once said you get much further with a gun and a smile than with a smile alone. Do you want to be someone who is constantly looking at a gun? I hope not.

18

Leaders Who Go Off the Deep End
Narcissism and Hubris

I see heads before my eyes that are ripe and ready for my sword to pluck them. And I see blood glistening between the turbans and the beards.[1]

     Al-Hadjadj bin Yuuf al-Thaqafi,
     Governor of Kufa and Basra (Iraq)

Some leaders go far beyond the abnormal ways of functioning we have looked at up till now. They go right off the deep end. We see this occasionally in business settings but more dramatically in the realm of politics, where the opportunities for excess are perhaps greater.

Iraq's Saddam Hussein, for example, exercises a leadership of excess. That he is a leader, and an effective one by some measures, is undeniable: he has charisma, energy, and the ability to inspire followers with drama. But when he invaded Kuwait in August 1990, he made the first move in a series of events that culminated in the Gulf War of 1991, which saw Iraq pitted against the massed power of an allied opposition led by the United States. Saddam Hussein's role as immediate instigator of the Gulf crisis led many people to question what kind of man he is.

Some political analysts have suggested that Saddam Hussein has simply gone crazy, that he is no longer in full possession of his senses. Others deny that there is anything wrong with him. They argue that he merely operates by a very different set of rules from those that govern minds brought up in Western societies. Actually, both camps may be partially right.

Whatever the case may be, Saddam Hussein brings us to the interesting question of what makes a leader go off the rails. What kind of psychological processes are at work when leaders start to act strange? What are the key factors that push a person over the brink? How does it happen, and where does it start?

A facetious commentator could argue that the recipe for insanity is relatively simple. First, and most important, one has to start early in life (the earlier, the better). Child psychologists have pointed out that the first three years of life are particularly critical to the development of an individual. These are the years during which the core patterns of personality are shaped; this is the period when we emerge as a person with a sense of our own body, name, mind, and personal history. As we saw in Chapter Seventeen, it is the period during which the foundations are laid for the kind of person we are going to be, the kind of person we are likely to remain for the rest of our life.

"Narcissistic development" is the clinical term for the influential changes that take place during an individual's early years of life. Narcissism is the engine that drives people. And narcissism and leadership are intricately connected.

A healthy dose of narcissism is essential for human functioning. However, the dangers of excess, particularly in the case of leaders, give narcissism its often derogatory connotation. We may be amused by Oscar Wilde's statement that "to love oneself is the beginning of a lifelong romance," but the bottom line is that the word *narcissism* evokes associations of egotism, self-centeredness, and exaggerated self-love. After all, who wants to be compared to that unfortunate young man, the Narcissus of Greek myth, who fell in love with his own reflection and pined to death?

Narcissism and hubris go hand in hand, and the hubris of leaders is all too familiar. Glory is a great temptress, but the pursuit of glory can be surprisingly self-destructive. The narcissistic pull is often so strong that no heed is paid to glory's dangers. Napoleon Bonaparte (an expert on this topic) once said, "Glory is fleeting, but obscurity lasts forever."

Narcissism (in its clinical meaning) refers to a stage of infantile development we all have to pass through, a stage during which the growing child derives pleasure from his or her own body and its functions. And this early stage is a very delicate time in the child's life. The kind of treatment received during this critical period colors a person's way of dealing with the world right through to adulthood.

The role of parents is obviously very important. Were they supportive and consistent? Or, at the other end of the scale, were family circumstances such that the child experienced a series of emotional deprivations? The key question becomes whether the child received adequate narcissistic supplies. Was a solid foundation laid for positive self-regard and initiative in establishing stable relationships? Did the child have the opportunity to acquire a healthy dose of self-esteem?

Given the human need for narcissistic supplies, it will not come as a surprise that many studies of successful leaders indicate that having a supportive mother is a great help. In my conversations with many successful leaders, one thing that stands out is that they feel they have had a privileged relationship with their mother. There is a lot of truth in Freud's famous statement that the child who has been the "mother's undisputed darling [will] retain throughout life the triumphant feeling, the confidence in success, which not seldom brings actual success along with it."

Of course, this does not mean that it is not important to have a supportive father around, but his presence is not as important as that of the mother. Napoleon may have exaggerated when he allegedly said, "The future destiny of the child is always the work of the mother," but to a certain extent the hand that rocks the cradle rules the world!

Narcissism is a strange thing, a double-edged sword. Having either too much or too little of it can throw a person off balance. When equilibrium is lost, instability may develop in the core of an individual's personality, because narcissistic elements help constitute the basis of self-esteem and identity.

Unfortunately, no parent is perfect. Becoming a person is not at all like that comfortable period of intrauterine existence when everything was automatically taken care of. In fact, growing up implies a certain amount of inevitable frustration. For normal development, however, frustration should occur in tolerable doses.

As a way of coping with the shortcomings of parental care, and in an attempt to ward off a sense of frustration, children like to retain the original impression of the perfection and bliss of the early years by creating both a grandiose, exhibitionistic image of their self and an all-powerful, idealized image of their parents (the latter taking on the role of saviors and protectors). Psychoanalysts call these two narcissistic configurations the "grandiose self" and the "idealized parent image." Over time, if children receive what we call "good-enough" care, these two configurations that make up the bipolar self are tamed by the forces of reality. Parents, siblings, and other important figures in a child's life modify the exhibitionistic displays, channeling grandiose fantasies of power and glory in proper directions, thus laying the foundation for realistic ambitions, stable values, well-defined career interests, and a secure sense of self-esteem and identity.

But not everyone is lucky enough to have a solid parental bond, one in which the parent recognizes the child's individuality and is able to bring to bear age-appropriate frustration. Many things can go wrong in the process of growing up. In some situations, prolonged disappointment due to parental overstimulation or understimulation or to highly inconsistent, arbitrary parental behavior leads to problems of a narcissistic nature. And if violence and abuse are part and parcel of the package, the stage is set for an inner theater complete with malevolent imagery. In the case of public figures, these scenes may be acted out on a world stage later in life.

The cartoonist Matt Groening once drew an illuminating but very disturbing cartoon. In the drawing is an extremely unhappy, monstrous-looking little child who has been tied up and locked in a cell. Two pairs of eyes are looking through the cell-door window, and the caption reads, "I hope you realize you're breaking our hearts." This cartoon, which portrays the alarmingly mixed signals given by some parents, is a good illustration of the kind of child-rearing that contributes to an unhealthy personality.

When good-enough care is absent, when frustration is handed out in improper doses, a child may experience this critical period in life with a great sense of deprivation. There may be a special bond with the mother, but sometimes this too comes at a heavy price. Some mothers—as we saw in the discussion of workaholics—can be quite devastating, burdening the child with a whale of a conscience; as a result, the child (and later the adult) never feels good enough. Other mothers send the child on a "mission impossible," hoping that he or she will take revenge for real or imagined wrongs they themselves suffered. Still others, crossing the fine line between support and smothering, are not able to give the child adequate psychic space.

Children who have been exposed to these types of parenting sometimes come to believe that they cannot reliably depend on anyone's love or loyalty. As adults, then, they act according to that conviction. These are people who, despite their claims to self-sufficiency, are troubled in the depth of their being by a sense of deprivation, anger, and emptiness. In order to cope with these feelings, and perhaps as a cover for their insecurity, they turn their narcissistic needs into obsessions. Such individuals become fixated on issues of power, beauty, status, prestige, and superiority. They try continually to maneuver others into strengthening their shaky sense of self-esteem. Some of them are also preoccupied with thoughts of getting even for the hurts (real or imagined) that they experienced during childhood.

My clinical work with leaders shows that a considerable percentage of them have become what they are for negative reasons.

Because of the hardships they have encountered, many of them seem to be on a mission: they are going to prove the world wrong; they are going to show everyone that they can amount to something. Many of them, suffering from what could be called the Count of Monte Cristo complex (after Alexander Dumas's novel) go even further: they have a very strong need to get even for the wrongs done to them at earlier periods in their lives.

Pierre Cardin, the French couturier, resembles someone with the Count of Monte Cristo complex. Growing up as an Italian young-ster in France, Cardin was teased by other children and called such names as "macaroni," all of which hurt. Second-class status is never easy to take. Cardin's family had lost most of its possessions during the war, and this had affected his father very badly; he drifted from job to job, adding to the sense of upheaval in the family. The young Cardin was kept going, in spite of all the turmoil around him, by the strong support of his mother. We can speculate, however, that this whole experience left Cardin with a sense of having to get back at his tormentors by amounting to something and to become the redeemer of the family. And he certainly did. Perhaps because once people had looked down at him and his family, he became a spe-cialist in leveling. He democratized fashion and brought haute cou-ture to the general public. At present, sales under his name amount to over $1 billion. Almost 200,000 people work for his label through more than 840 licensing arrangements in 125 countries. He has put his name on everything imaginable. He even thumbed his nose at the French aristocracy by buying the famous restaurant Maxim, once their favorite watering hole.[2] Now Maxim has been democra-tized; you can eat there with salespeople from Cleveland!

As Pierre Cardin's example illustrates, narcissism is not neces-sarily a bad thing; it can lead to considerable success. For people in positions of leadership, a healthy dose of narcissism is very impor-tant. Narcissism is the engine that drives people to participate in political and organizational life. It is the motivating force that makes things happen. This constructive form of narcissism, based on a secure sense of self-esteem and identity and a clear understanding of who one is and what one is able to do, goes a long way in leadership.

Narcissists of this type have the capacity for introspection. In addition, they radiate a sense of positive vitality and are capable of empathetic feelings. This is in complete contrast to dysfunctional or "reactive" narcissists, who are continually trying to boost a defective sense of self-esteem and are preoccupied with emotions such as envy, spite, revenge, and vindictive triumph over others. This latter group, as I have indicated, may have been exposed to inconsistent, perhaps highly disturbing patterns of childrearing. As a caveat, it should be said that there exists a subgroup among reactive narcissists. People in this subgroup are able to transcend the urge to get even. In fact, they want to repair. Because they do not want others to have to go through the same experiences they did, they do not adopt a vindictive mode. Instead, their behavior is more like that of the constructive narcissists. Acting in positive, helpful ways becomes their method of mastering past hurts.

How can we recognize the dysfunctional reactive narcissists? Let us look at some of the indicators. To begin with, these people tend to have a grandiose sense of self-importance. They habitually take advantage of others in order to achieve their own ends. They also live under the illusion that they are special, that their problems are unique. In addition, they feel a sense of entitlement; they believe that they deserve especially favorable treatment and that the rules set for others do not apply to them. Furthermore, they are addicted to compliments; they can never get enough. Lacking empathy, they are unable to experience how others feel. Last but certainly not least, their envy of others, and their rage when prevented from getting their own way, can be formidable.

In the molding of leaders, the climb to the top usually involves a lengthy period of subordination and forced deference, a time during which people have to learn how to control and focus their otherwise blind ambition. This is difficult for those who have problems centered on narcissism. If they are going to succeed, they may have to disguise their real nature; they may need a capacity for acting, for assuming a role.

Suppose the charm—false or otherwise—of certain aspiring leaders pays off. Suppose their playacting finally enables them to reach the top position. What happens next?

Unfortunately, as many leaders have found out, being on top is not necessarily a bed of roses. Along with the perks comes a great deal of pressure. In addition, leaders must deal with the loneliness of command. The moment one becomes top dog, the network of old relationships is disturbed. Every move one makes now has a great deal of symbolism attached to it. Leaders who have to make critical decisions about people's future cannot be as close to old colleagues as they once were. Whether new leaders like it or not, some distance has to be kept. Distance is not always easy, however. After all, leaders have their own dependency needs. Who is going to take care of them? This issue can cause a considerable amount of stress and frustration.

Then there is the troublesome problem of envy. Many people look at the power and trappings of leadership and become envious. Because the envy of others can be extremely disturbing, it may awaken dormant feelings of paranoia in leaders. In paranoid thinking, illusions of grandeur and delusions of persecution go hand in hand. There is the fear—not always unreasonable—that others will try to take away what it cost the leaders so much effort to gain. The fear of losing the power of office can put a debilitating strain on leaders. They become, as it were, afraid of success. They may become depressed as well, seemingly paralyzed by the demands of decision making.

Other narcissistically rooted problems faced by leaders also involve people lower in the hierarchy. One that is of particular importance concerns the complicated question of transference. I will try to make clear what this is all about.

Let us again consider the grandiose self and the idealized parental image, which I discussed earlier in this essay in the context of the development of self-esteem. Since each of us has had experiences with these narcissistic configurations, remnants of the feelings they engendered linger on in all of us. These feelings can once again come alive vis-à-vis people in a position of authority.

In dealing with authority figures, people can become emotionally confused in terms of time and place. In the phenomenon that Freud described as a "false connection," followers do not perceive and respond to their leader according to the reality of the situation but as if the leader were a significant figure from the past (such as a parent or other authoritative person). Also known as transference, this ubiquitous element of the human condition is a way in which we process information and organize experience. It is a strange but nevertheless very real mechanism: the emotional legacy of the past pushes followers into displacing many of their historic hopes and fantasies onto the present leader. A good indication of the presence of transferential responses are instances when an individual's reactions to persons or situations seem too intense, inappropriate, or overly emotional.

One regular pattern is the desire on the part of followers to please their leader and a willingness to do anything to achieve that goal. This need to idealize is likely to meet with a very receptive response, particularly from someone with a narcissistic personality. Leaders of this type welcome the outpouring of applause and admiration. Indeed, they may arrive at the stage where they cannot function without this kind of emotional fix. Of course, it is possible for this kind of admiration to create a lot of energy in the system, and idealization can be useful in aligning and energizing subordinates in order to enact a common vision. But the leader's ability to transform what were once only fantasies into reality adds to the heady experience of being on top. This feeling of specialness may cause the leader to lose a sense of the boundaries of what is appropriate behavior. Leaders may come to think that the rules pertinent to others do not apply to them.

The saga of Jacques Attali, the former president and creator of the European Bank for Reconstruction and Development, is a good illustration of what can happen when narcissism goes to a person's head. He is an example of a person, seduced by the sirens of narcissism, who ignored the rules of behavior applicable to common mortals. Not only was Attali accused by Nobel Prize winner Elie Wiesel of plagiarism (in Attali's latest book, he appropriated a number of Wiesel's conversations with the French president Mitterrand and claimed they were his own); he found himself in a maelstrom of his own making over his leadership of his London-based bank.

Attali's appointment as head of the bank was controversial from the beginning, because he had no previous banking experience and had never been an administrator. It was generally acknowledged, however, that he was very intelligent and was experienced in politics. The enthusiasm and persuasion that had made him the driving force behind the conception of the bank seemed to make him the obvious choice for the presidency. Indeed, his tenure began well, according to an *Economist* article of April 18, 1992:

> The EBRD makes a cautious beginning, as its leader gets some high marks. . . . Some critics have been won over by the bank's high-profile president, Jacques Attali. . . . Further, Attali has forged unexpected cooperation with the owners of the bank, 54 nations and 2 institutions based in Europe.

Attali soon found himself in the center of controversy at the bank, however, because of his imperious, arrogant behavior. The journal *Euromoney* included the following comments in its April 1992 issue:

> Despite Attali's vision and intellectual gifts, there are doubts about his suitability to head a large international bank and his abilities as a manager and motivator of people. His management style is to keep as much as possible in his own hands. Formal management structures at the

EBRD mean little, with the real center of power being
Attali's cabinet.

Attali's name quickly became synonymous with a culture of
extravagance. The EBRD's mandate to foster democracies and promote the private sector in the ruined command economies of Eastern Europe seemed to become an afterthought in Attali's search for
glory. He dropped the names of the rich and famous, often bragging
that he was on a first-name basis with forty-seven heads of state. He
behaved as though he owned the bank, and his high-handed behavior was reflected in his leadership style, which was autocratic and
secretive. This soon led to political infighting among his subordinates
and created a climate of fear and an absence of dissent. As time went
by, more energy was spent on politics than on the business at hand.

The drama reached its denouement when the July 24, 1993,
Financial Times disclosed that the bank had spent twice as much on
refurbishing its head office as it had on loans to Eastern Europe.
Attali's office suite was described as being worthy of a Greek ship-
ping magnate, with three antechambers, a private bathroom, mir-
rored ceilings, a deep white rug, and spectacular views of the city.
Moreover, revelations emerged about financial improprieties on the
part of Attali, such as double-billing the bank for travel expenses.
According to the *Times* article, the journal *France-Soir* summarized
the situation neatly:

> Attali, Jacques. Graduate of the École Polytechnique,
> the School of Mines, Sciences Politiques, the National
> School of Administration (ENA), Ph.D. in Economics.
> The finest collection of degrees in the Republique. A
> head, a brain, a machine for thinking . . . Jacques Attali.
> Delirium. Megalomania.

Eventually, the bank's board of governors, embarrassed by the
persistent bad press, had had enough of the situation and pushed

Attali to resign. On July 16, 1993, the bank published a damning report on Attali's lavish spending and his questionable use of credit cards and private jets. Attali left the bank that day, without waiting for the arrival of a successor as he had originally intended. In addition, he waived more than $220,000 in termination allowance in exchange for the promise that no claims for expenses would be brought against him in the future.

From Attali's comments to the press, it appears that he did not learn much from his brief tenure at the EBRD. He showed little remorse, as is often the case with narcissistically oriented people. It is obvious, however, that it was his arrogant, imperious behavior that led to his downfall.

As the case of Attali illustrates, leaders are very susceptible to finding themselves in a hall of mirrors, seeing and hearing only what they want to. And even worse, if people do not oblige them—if followers are unwilling to share their distorted view of the world—they may throw tantrums, reenacting patterns of childhood behavior. Some of these narcissistic leaders perceive noncompliance as a direct attack on the very essence of their personality, given their fragile sense of self-esteem. Past feelings of helplessness and humiliation may be revived, leading to blind rage. However, *this* time, given the power they wield, their tantrums make a great difference.

The impact of this rage on their immediate environment can be devastating. The majority of their followers, torn between love and fear, generally submit to the demands put upon them. They become handy scapegoats on which to enact group revenge when things do not go the way the leader wants—tangible entities on which to project everything of which the leader is afraid, everything that is perceived by the leader as evil and threatening to the system. This kind of development can have terrifying results. In the case of a corporate leader such as Robert Maxwell, it can lead to the complete destruction of an organization, while in the case of a national leader such as Saddam Hussein, it can affect an entire country. The behavior of both Maxwell and Hussein makes us reflect on the words of George Bernard Shaw, who once said that every despot must have one disloyal subject to keep him sane.

19

Conclusion

In Praise of a Little Madness

Every man has a sane spot somewhere.
Robert Louis Stevenson

We are all born mad. Some remain so.
Samuel Beckett

Better mad with the rest of the world than wise alone.
Balthasar Gracian

A recurring theme throughout this collection of essays is the idea that leaders and followers are all too often irrational and illogical. I realize that in writing about executive behavior, dysfunctional leadership, and organizational pathology—even about everyday business practices such as downsizing and cross-cultural management—I discourage or depress people at times. Recognizing ineffective or dysfunctional patterns in oneself or one's organization can be quite disconcerting. There are certainly times when even I like to be equipped with rose-colored glasses!

A question I am often asked is, "What, then, is the 'normal' person like?" When this question is raised, I usually turn to Freud, who once was presented with a similar question by a journalist. As the story goes, the journalist, who had expected a long, convoluted answer, was very surprised at Freud's response: a healthy person is someone who is capable of both *Liebe und Arbeit*, who has a capacity for both love and work. (A workaholic himself, Freud did not mention the concept of *homo ludens:* he did not talk about our ability to play!)

The conciseness of Freud's answer, however, does not detract from its richness. His words refer to the question of human connectedness, the ease or difficulty with which individuals establish relationships and have empathetic feelings for others. And of course the major human connections involve love (in its broadest sense) and work. To what extent do we have the capacity for intimacy and reciprocity, the ability to establish and maintain long-term relationships in both domains of human functioning? As a corollary, to what extent do we experience a sense of belonging, of being part of a group and being satisfied in a social context? Do we have someone to turn to for advice and help? Do we have a feeling of being needed?

Although the capacity for intimacy and reciprocity and a sense of belonging are major cornerstones of mental health, is there anything to be added to Freud's comment about love and work? What are some of the other indicators of mental health?

The answers to these questions about mental health are important even in a book centered around life in organizations. After all, a considerable part of each person's life is spent at work. And if we want to achieve effective organizational functioning, it is essential that we identify people who possess a sound mental balance. Moreover, we should also be aware of the occurrence of stress symptoms in organizations. We should be on the lookout for the danger signs of executive malfunctioning and be able to recognize when executives have problems. Furthermore, we should know about ways of helping these people. (Of course, we should also be able to recognize stress symptoms in ourselves.) Consequently, identification of the various elements that make up mental health becomes a sine qua non.

To begin with the obvious, one very important criterion of mental health and normality is whether we possess a stable identity, a secure sense of self-esteem. Although it may be difficult to imagine, some people are not sure that they are not Jesus Christ, Napoleon, or Marilyn Monroe!

What about the capacity for reality testing? Do we have a good sense of what is going on around us, or do we tend to distort information? Do we censor what we do not like to see? Do we ignore unpleasant realities? Do we try to rewrite history?

Our psychological defense mechanisms can be a good indication of our state of mental health as well. How do we deal with conflicts? Are our impulses and emotions kept under control? Are our defenses primitive or sophisticated? Everybody needs some defenses, of course; without defense mechanisms, we would all be psychotic. Some people, however, get trapped by their defenses, losing flexibility in the way they use them. As I indicated in the examples of Saddam Hussein and Robert Maxwell, splitting is a good example of a primitive defensive reaction. People who resort to splitting do not have the ability to see nuances; they constantly divide the world into good and bad, cops and robbers, madonnas and prostitutes. Such persons lack the capacity to tolerate ambivalence; they cannot accept that individuals can be *both* good and bad. (Actually, if we delve a little bit deeper into the matter, we discover that such individuals are compelled to deny the badness they perceive in their own personalities but are quite ready to attribute badness to others.)

Many people use other primitive defenses, such as denial and projection. Having never really overcome their childlike ways, they are driven to repeat behavior patterns from childhood. For example, when a parent comes home and—finding the house a wreck—cries out, "Who made this mess?" the guilty child commonly says, "I didn't do it; he did!" This is a good illustration of denial and projection in action. Such behavior patterns may be understandable in small children, but with adults we should have higher expectations for mental functioning. It should be possible for adults to take responsibility for their actions.

Unfortunately, too many adults go through life with preferred defense mechanisms of a primitive nature. Such people always deny *any* responsibility for their actions. Things are *never* their fault; it is always someone else who is to blame. Other individuals obey any order from an authority figure (remember those who appease the aggressor?), with occasionally dire results. We need only think of the atrocities that take place during wars.

In this context, the theme of self-protection should be mentioned. I am not preaching about the virtues of negativism, nor am I holding up as models people who are passive-aggressive. It is, however, important for us to know when to say no. We need to realize when boundaries are being transgressed. Extreme compliance and obedience are not signs of mental health. An infant or small child may not have much of a choice, but when we reach a certain stage of personal development, we have to protect ourselves; we have to know where the limits are. Certainly, instructions that could be life-threatening should not be followed; and if someone orders us to do something that may cause harm to others or ourselves, we should be able at least to ask why.

Another criterion of mental health is our outlook on control. How controlling are we? Can we express our need for control in a constructive way, or do we experience an overwhelming desire to exert power and control in all aspects of life, stifling others in their development and ordering everybody around?

Still another important criterion of mental health is whether we can experience the whole range of emotions. Can we really feel, and do we *know* when we feel mad, sad, bad, or glad? Surprising as it may sound, some people do not. Remember the alexithymics— those who seem to be color-blind as far as their emotions are concerned? I have had male executives in my programs say quite seriously that they depend on their wives to tell them how they feel!

Other factors include the capacity for impulse control. How able are we to tolerate frustration? Can we handle anger and anxiety, or do these feelings run out of control? Can we control our sexual desires? Do we belong to that group of people who may become abusive? And what about our capacity for dealing with depression? As we all know, life is full of stressful events. How well do we cope with these setbacks?

Do we have the ability to mourn? When faced with serious set-backs, do we tend to fall apart, to break down? How mature are we in dealing with separation? Are we too dependent; do we, in difficult situations, become clingy and hold on, or can we let go? Can we work through personal losses and psychologically come to grips with them?

And what about sublimatory channels? To what extent can we modify instinctual impulses (such as aggression) into more acceptable, nonconflictual activities (such as artistic creation, work, sports, humor, and so on)? Are we able to "regress in the service of the ego"—to be playful and constructive in expressing pleasurable fantasies and wishes?

There are still other conditions that indicate mental health or imbalance, among which are conceptions of body image and body functioning. To what extent are we preoccupied with our physical appearance? Are we satisfied with how we look, or are our looks an endless preoccupation? An extreme case of body image dysfunction is seen in anorexics, who have a completely distorted perception of their body; they do not realize that they are starving themselves. Where others see an emaciated person, they see someone who is heavily overweight.

Preoccupation with body functioning is a related criterion. For some people, body functioning becomes the center of attention. Talking about their digestive system, their lungs, their heart, their sinuses becomes an end in itself. Normal conversation is no longer possible; every discussion ends up centered around such a topic. Understandably, we see more of this as people begin to age.

When considering physiology and its role in mental health, sexual functioning and satisfaction should not be forgotten. Do we experience problems with sexual functioning? Are we inhibited, anxious, or malfunctioning? What about sexual satisfaction? Does our sex life give pleasure? These are very private questions, far from the normal realm of organizational life—not the kind of questions one can raise in polite conversation!—but they are very important.

In addition to these criteria of mental health, several serious psychological warning signs should be mentioned. For example, strong feelings of self-rejection and self-hate may indicate deeply damaged self-esteem and should be a cause for worry. So too with a sense of personal worthlessness. Moreover, the conviction that one's feelings of worthlessness are noticeable to others adds to the problem. For individuals troubled in this way, Sartre's remark that hell is other people is sadly true.

There are also people who experience a desperate longing to be loved, a feeling that coexists with the conviction that they are unlovable. Such people may constantly suffer from the fear of rejection. Others are bothered by feelings of loneliness and not belonging. These are people who may experience chronic problems with intimacy.

Last but not least, the fear of having a mental illness is an ominous sign that something may be wrong, as are chronic (but often suppressed) feelings of anger, resentment, guilt, hostility, and depression. Very worrisome is the feeling—one that some people take with them through life—that something inside one has died.

In theory, the healthy individual is able to recognize, and attempt to confront, any of the above indications in his or her own psyche. In other words, the ability to observe and analyze oneself is of primary importance. Realistically, however, most people (executives are prime examples) have a tendency to run all the time. This phenomenon can be described as the "manic" defense. People who cannot sit still, either physically or mentally, have little capacity to stand back and reflect on their actions. It is as if they were afraid that they might not like what they would find if they opened their own Pandora's box.

Where do we go from here, given all these concerns about what the healthy, "normal" individual is like? In perusing a checklist such as this, *every* reader can easily find something wrong. This does not mean that we should all be dashing immediately to a psychiatrist or psychoanalyst, however.

Is being a truly "normal" person really something to strive for anyway? I hope not. We all have our warts, and we should learn to live with them. Some cultures, including that of the British, favor their eccentrics. Indeed, one could argue that the person who has a self-declared normal personality may be the sickest of us all! Nothing is so disturbing as dealing with the "normopath." Some of the normopaths I have met are truly devoid of life. They are incapable of nonconformism. In these people, the ability to surprise and a sense of wonder (so important if we want to feel alive) seem to be missing. In addition, the creative spark may be lacking. The Spanish Nobel laureate Camilo Jose Cela once wrote, "The healthy man has no ideas. I sometimes think that religious, moral, social, and political ideas are nothing but manifestations of an imbalance in the nervous system."

I hope it is clear by now that the difference between health and sickness depends on one's position on a spectrum of health and pathology. I argue that it is only the extreme positions on this spectrum that are a cause for worry and that may result in a range of dysfunctional behavior, from ineffective leadership to crazy leadership, as we have discussed. To recognize true dysfunctionality in oneself may cause problems and lead to some discomfort. Apart from the extremes, however, I hope that we can all accept that we need a little madness in life. Actually, those who accept the madness in themselves may be the healthiest of all. But as the family therapist Carl Whittaker once said, "Most of us do not have the courage to be crazy except in the middle of the night when we are sound asleep, and we try to forget it before we wake up."

Notes

· ·

Preface

1. A. Jardim, *The First Henry Ford: A Study in Personality and Business Leadership* (Cambridge, Mass.: MIT Press, 1970); and R. Lacey, *Ford: The Men and the Machine* (Boston, Mass.: Little, Brown, 1986).

Chapter Two

1. "Lou Gerstner's First 30 Days," *Fortune*, May 31, 1993, pp. 56–60.

2. R. F. Vancil, *Passing the Baton* (Boston, Mass.: Harvard Business School Press, 1987).

Chapter Three

1. "Case Zeiss Jena: Managing Catastrophe." INSEAD case number 12/92–258. © 1992 Manfred Kets de Vries.

2. N. M. Tichy and S. Sherman, *Control Your Destiny or Someone Else Will* (New York: Doubleday, 1993); and R. Slater, *The New GE* (Homewood, Ill.: Business One Irwin, 1993).

Chapter Four

1. M. L. Marks and P. Mirvis, "Merger Syndrome: Stress and Uncertainty," *Mergers and Acquisitions*, Summer 1985, pp. 50–55; C. D. Siehl, D. Smith, and A. Omura, "After the Merger: Should Executives Stay or Go?" *Academy of Management Executive* 4, no. 1 (1990): 50–60; and P. Haspeslagh and D. B. Jamieson, *Managing*

Acquisitions (New York: Free Press, 1991).

Chapter Seven

1. A. Zaleznik, M.F.R. Kets de Vries, and J. Howard, "Stress Reactions in Organizations: Syndromes, Causes, and Consequences," *Behavioral Science* 22, no. 3 (1977): 151–162.

2. N. Adler, *International Dimensions of Organizational Behavior* (Boston, Mass.: Ken Publishing, 1986); and R. Tung, "Selection and Training of Personnel for Overseas Assignments," *Columbia Journal of World Business* 16, no. 1 (1981): 68–78.

3. N. Adler, *International Dimensions of Organizational Behavior* (Boston, Mass.: Ken Publishing, 1986); and M. Mendenhall, E. Dunbar, and G. R. Oddou, "Expatriate Selection, Training, and Career Pathing: A Review and Critique," *Human Resource Management* 26, no. 3 (1987): 331–345.

Chapter Eight

1. J. Bowlby, *Attachment and Loss*, vol. 1 (New York: Basic Books, 1969).

Chapter Nine

1. H. Mintzberg, *Mintzberg on Management: Inside Our Strange World of Organizations* (New York: Free Press, 1989).

Chapter Ten

1. J. Fierman, "Do Women Manage Differently?" *Fortune*, Dec. 17, 1990, p. 71.

Chapter Eleven

1. T. J. Watson, Jr., and P. Petre, *Father, Son, & Co.: My Life at IBM and Beyond* (New York: Bantam, 1990), pp. vii, 342.

2. M.F.R. Kets de Vries, "The Dynamics of Family-Controlled Firms," *Organizational Dynamics*, Winter 1993, pp. 59–71; and M.F.R. Kets

de Vries, *Human Dilemmas in Family Firms: A Case Book* (London: Routledge, forthcoming).

3. M. Zeitlin, "Corporate Ownership and Control," *American Journal of Sociology* 79 (1976): 1073–1119; and R. Donckels and E. Fröhlich, "Are Family Businesses Really Different? European Experiences from Stratos," *Family Business Review* 4, no. 2 (1991): 149–160.

4. R. Beckhard and W. G. Dyer, "Managing Change in Family Firms: Issues and Strategies," *Sloan Management Review* 24 (1983): 54–65; and W. G. Dyer, *Cultural Change in Family Firms: Anticipating and Managing Business and Family Transitions* (San Francisco: Jossey-Bass, 1986).

5. R. Poe, "The SOBs," *Across the Board*, May 1980, pp. 23–33.

Chapter Twelve

1. G. Wallas, *The Art of Thought* (Orlando, Fla.: Harcourt, Brace, Jovanovich, 1926).

2. W. Niederland and S. Bahman, *The Creative Process: A Psychoanalytic Discussion* (New York: Concourse Press, 1982).

Chapter Thirteen

1. R. F. Vancil, *Passing the Baton* (Boston, Mass.: Harvard Business School Press, 1987).

Chapter Fourteen

1. J. Howard, D. Cunningham, and P. Rechnitzer, *Rusting Out, Burning Out, Bowing Out: Stress and Survival on the Job* (Toronto: Macmillan of Canada, 1978).

2. C. Cordes, "Type A Children: Anxious, Insecure," *APA Monitor* 16, no. 11 (1985): 20.

Chapter Fifteen

1. P. E. Sifneos, "The Prevalence of Alexithymic Characteristics in Psychosomatic Patients," *Psychotherapy and Psychosomatics* 22, no. 6 (1973): 255–262.

2. J. McDougall, *Theaters of the Body* (New York: Norton, 1989).

Chapter Sixteen

1. T. Bower, *Maxwell: The Outsider* (London: Mandarin Paperbacks, 1992), p. 511.

2. Information in the Robert Maxwell case study was derived from the Bower work cited in the previous note and from P. Thompson and A. Delano, *Maxwell: A Portrait of Power* (London: Corgi, 1988).

3. R. Cohen, "Robert Maxwell's Last, Isolated Days," *International Herald Tribune*, Dec. 21–22, 1991, p. 11.

4. Ibid., p. 13.

Chapter Eighteen

1. A. Darwish and G. Alexander, *Unholy Babylon* (London: Victor Gollancz, 1991), p. 93.

2. R. Morais, *Pierre Cardin: The Man Who Became a Label* (London: Bankim Press, 1991).

Index